"In *Create More,* Len Jessup condenses a lifetime of lessons he has learned about leadership and entrepreneurship into a concise, readable guide to inspire both emerging and seasoned leaders. He invokes visionary leaders like Steve Jobs to bolster his bullet points that are certain to advance the creativity, vision, charisma, drive, and resilience of effective leaders. As a university president committed to more entrepreneurial approaches, I appreciate Len's insights and am certain that leaders of all types of organizations and institutions stand to benefit from this timely work."

— Michael M. Crow, President, Arizona State University

The visionary behind the university's transformation into the nation's most innovative educational institutions

"I've known Len Jessup since he tapped me to be on his business college board at Washington State University and have had the opportunity to watch his progress through subsequent education-leadership roles. I saw the definition of entrepreneurial leadership close up as it unfolded through deanships, presidencies, and now investment guidance in the business community. It's been fun to see his leadership in action. This book's subtitle references 'life at the edge of entrepreneurship,' but more accurately Len has been immersed at the heart of entrepreneurship."

—Mike Flynn, Former Publisher of the Puget Sound Business Journal

Built the regional business media outlet into one of the nation's most respected platforms

"I've known Len Jessup here in the Las Vegas Valley for well over a decade, first as UNLV president and now as managing partner for Desert Forge Ventures. Len's new book, *Create More*, captures well the entrepreneurial spirit needed not only for founders of new ventures, but also for leaders in large, mature organizations as well. Len's got the entrepreneurial spirit as well, and he does it with warmth and humor."

—Diana Bennett, Gaming Hall of Fame Inductee
Led Paragon Gaming into a cross-border hospitality powerhouse

"Len has had a front row seat to the western US region's evolution into technology transfer and academic-led entrepreneurship. He has popped up at major universities at the precise moment commercialization began. Much of that timing is his own doing as a passionate leader in navigating the complexities of moving university-led research to the world's markets. His retirement plan is to launch a venture capital firm dedicated to Nevada's emerging tech transfer ecosystem. Len, welcome to the jungle!"

—Fletcher J. McCusker, Founder/CEO of Providence and UArizona Venture Capital
Turned a $50K startup into Tucson's first billion-dollar public company

CREATE MORE

CREATE MORE

LESSONS LEARNED
FROM A LIFE AT THE EDGE
OF ENTREPRENEURSHIP,
IN FIVE ACTS

LEN JESSUP, PhD

Entrepreneur | Books

Published by Entrepreneur® Books, Charleston, South Carolina.
An imprint of Advantage Media Group.

Printed in the United States of America.

10 9 8 7 6 5 4 3 2 1

ISBN: 979-8-89701-015-8 (Paperback)
ISBN: 979-8-89701-016-5 (eBook)

Library of Congress Control Number: 2025917350

08-08-2025 12:33

To Roger Girard, mentor, partner, friend, and a model of fearless, selfless, entrepreneurial leadership, whose steady hand, sharp eye, and generous heart have guided so many ventures, including mine.

CONTENTS

PROLOGUE

I'VE ALWAYS BEEN FASCINATED by entrepreneurial leaders. Many of them come to mind across nearly every business sector. Take, for example, Steve Jobs, Bill Gates, and Elon Musk in tech; Howard Schultz, Phil Knight, or Estée Lauder in consumer products and retail; Henry Ford and Thomas Edison in industrial and automotive; and Oprah Winfrey or Walt Disney in media and entertainment. These entrepreneurs share qualities such as vision, risk-taking, persistence, and the ability to adapt to changing markets. Whether in technology, retail, or media, their leadership reshaped their respective industries and created enduring legacies.

Let's take a closer look at Steve Jobs and, in particular, the effect that leaders like him have on people around them. The impact that Jobs had on people inside Apple is legendary. His influence was so strong that it was referred to as a reality distortion field, a term that is thought to have first been used by Bud Tribble at Apple Computer in the early 1980s to describe company cofounder Jobs's formidable charisma and the effect that it had on those he worked with. Tribble reportedly said that the term came from an episode of *Star Trek* titled "The Menagerie." In that episode, the aliens encountered by the crew of the starship *Enterprise* could create their own new world simply through mental force (Isaacson 2011).

In Jobs's case, it might have been a combination of charisma, influence, or just sheer force of will, but there is plenty of evidence to show that he had a strong, persuasive effect on people around him. His energy was infectious, his way of thinking was contagious, and for whatever reason, people believed him, were inspired by him, and wanted to follow him (Gallo 2009). That's amazing, considering that, early on, he was selling something that sounded outlandish and so far off in the future!

Early in his career, Jobs and Apple cofounder Steve Wozniak were trying to sell a vision for a personal computer that was unlike anything commercially available at the time. Many don't realize that at least some of Jobs's vision was inspired by a fortuitous visit he and others from Apple made across town at the Xerox Palo Alto Research Center (PARC) in 1979. They observed groundbreaking innovations at Xerox's innovation lab that significantly influenced the development of the early Macintosh computer. Some key examples of technologies they saw at PARC and later adapted included the graphical user interface (GUI) to organize your computer's virtual desktop, the mouse as a pointing device, what you see is what you get (WYSIWYG) editing capabilities, networking among computers locally and with other devices, and object-oriented programming that made coding much easier and more intuitive.

That visit and its impact on Apple is well documented, and my point here is that the executives at Xerox *chose* not to commercialize those great ideas, and/or they tried to and were not able to commercialize them as successfully as Jobs did. Similarly, Wozniak is a genius in many ways, but he clearly did not become the face of Apple, and he isn't thought to be a passionate technology evangelist like his partner Jobs.

So, why is that? The team at PARC could have shaped history but didn't. Wozniak could have taken the mantle more publicly and become even more legendary, but he didn't. Jobs did. Why?

Jobs recognized the incredible commercial potential of those ideas and convinced his team members to implement them in a way that transformed the personal computing industry. The Macintosh, released in 1984, was one of the first widely available computers with a GUI, mouse, and WYSIWYG capabilities, setting new standards for usability and design.

Similarly, Jobs was able to convince investors and early adopters that his vision for a beautiful, natural, organic, and easy-to-use personal computer was better. He was an incredible combination of personal characteristics, including being visionary, smart, convincing, capable, and having unmatched drive and energy. He was, in short, an entrepreneurial leader (Addy et al. 2024).

Five Characteristics of Entrepreneurial Leaders

Let's go back to basics and consider some related fundamental definitions from Oxford Languages. An entrepreneur is a person who organizes and operates a business and takes on greater-than-normal financial risks to do so. Fair enough; but that's a lean definition, and it doesn't completely explain an entrepreneur like Steve Jobs and his success. We need to go well beyond that simple definition and expand it with five characteristics.

Characteristic #1: Creativity: I think of creativity as the use of original ideas or a clever mix of existing ideas. We typically think of creativity in the production of an artistic work, but it can span many other domains and ways of thinking. In Jobs's case, he very creatively perceived a way of combining a host of innovations he was seeing and sensing and pulling them all together in one elegant computer on a desktop. We can also say that while he was inspired by other innovations that he saw others produce, he saw a way to pull them all together with mixes of his own thinking in an original, advanced design and approach (West and Richter 2024). He also created an environment for it. Research shows that the most innovative leaders actively create environments that foster creativity and encourage experimentation rather than simply waiting for a moment of inspiration (Amabile 1997). Jobs was clearly an innovator thinking in novel, new ways.

Characteristic #2: Vision: Even more to the point, I think it is fair to say that Jobs was a visionary. We usually think of a visionary as someone who can think about or plan for the future with imagination or wisdom. In fact, we often say that many successful entrepreneurs can see potential in a market that doesn't yet exist and/or that others can't or won't see. We describe them as being imaginative, inventive, insightful, perceptive, intuitive, farsighted, prescient, and sometimes even idealistic or romantic in their visions of the future (Priyaa et al. 2025). Jobs was all of that and was a person who could *see around corners* in terms of future technology and our desire and need for it. That explains a lot for Jobs, but it doesn't completely explain his success.

Characteristic #3: Charisma: We mentioned Jobs's strong, forceful charisma, and so perhaps that is the missing ingredient. He was so charismatic that his colleagues gave it a name: *reality distortion field*. Very successful entrepreneurs are also able to convince, cajole, sway, or, in some other way, persuade others (Antonakis et al. 2016).

That's a key ingredient in our definition, and it's clearly a component of what makes these people strong and successful leaders. In my prior book, *Self Less*, I defined leadership at its most fundamental level as the ability of a person to influence the thoughts and/or actions of others in intended ways. That's at the core of Jobs's most basic talents.

Characteristic #4: Drive: I would add one more distinguishing characteristic of Jobs, and that was his indomitable drive. People like him have that strong internal motivation that pushes them to take action to achieve a goal (Hmieleski and Carr 2007). If vision is what sets the direction, then drive is the engine that gets you there. It's what pushes leaders to keep building when others quit. You can think of it as a strong desire to satisfy an urgent need, such as hunger or thirst. Just like you and I have a powerful daily need to eat, drink, or sleep, Jobs had an intense need to fulfill his vision of an elegant personal computer on every desktop and later to change the way we consume music, enjoy movies, and more. He lived it 24 hours a day, 7 days a week, and 365 days a year, felt it in the depths of his soul, and never shied away from it, perhaps to the detriment of his family life and ultimately even his own health.

Characteristic #5: Resilience: The visions that great entrepreneurs are chasing are often complicated and difficult and have huge barriers, pushback, and setbacks. Their desire for what is on the other side of these brick walls is so intense that they'll stop at nothing to go over, around, or through the walls to get to it. When knocked down, they find a way to get back up, dust themselves off, and continue to fight for what they want (Fisher, Maritz, and Lobo 2016; Hmieleski, Carr, and Baron 2015). Even the most visionary, driven leaders face setbacks—and that's where resilience comes in. It's the ability to get knocked down and still find the strength to get back up, adjust course, and keep going. Jobs was a good example of this. He was literally kicked out of his own company and then asked to come back and help save it.

What can we learn from the example of Jobs? He was a great example of the entrepreneurial leader that I am so interested in: the creative and innovative visionary, willing to take risks, able to turn their vision into sound plans and then into action, who is also very good at persuading others to follow them, either by working and/or by simply setting an example, with an intense drive to see their vision come to fruition and the resilience to continue in the face of strong adversity (Gupta et al. 2004; Renko et al. 2015).

These same traits are especially vital in high-tech industries, where things change quickly and the old leadership playbook just doesn't cut it. A recent review by Addy and colleagues (2024) looked closely at what makes entrepreneurial leaders successful in these high-stakes environments. Leaders who thrive in these spaces excel at spotting opportunities, fostering a culture of experimentation, encouraging cross-functional collaboration, and adapting to shifting technologies and markets. On a personal level, the best of them lead with emotional intelligence, communicate clearly, and know how to inspire people to take bold steps with them. That blend of strategic foresight and adaptability is what allows them to build teams and organizations that can keep innovating and growing—especially when the pressure is on.

CREATE MORE LESSON:

Entrepreneurial leaders are creative, visionary risk-takers, who are able to turn their visions into plans and then into actions, are very good at persuading others to follow them through drive and charisma, and have strong resilience in the face of adversity.

I don't claim to be like Steve Jobs, but thinking of him as an entrepreneurial leader reminds me of a time in my professional life when I felt like I was part of something special that seemed much like Jobs's early days at Apple. In the very early 2000s, another friend and I had been recruited by a long-standing, very talented, and charismatic mutual friend and colleague of ours to join him at Washington State University (WSU) to build a world-class program in management information systems (MIS). We had been able to participate in the very early efforts to build online programs at the Kelley School of Business at Indiana University prior to that, and we wanted to bring that innovative thinking in online education to WSU as well.

We recruited many other friends and colleagues to join us in our pursuit of innovation and excellence. We not only built a world-class program, placing many undergrads and grad students in great jobs all around the world, but we also built an incredible online undergrad degree in MIS, which was among the first of its kind in an accredited business school. We went on to help establish an online undergraduate degree in general business as well, and both programs did well and paved the way for the eventual launch of an online MBA, which became successful and was later ranked number one in the country.

We had a blast doing all of that early-stage work together, and we all look back on those days as our Camelot in our professional lives. I feel that my participation in that entire effort, dubbed MIS@ WSU, was about as close to entrepreneurial leadership as I've come in my professional life in higher education. In that case, our mutual friend was the entrepreneurial leader, and I was simply a competent manager/administrator by his side. In any event, it was exhilarating!

So that's the focus of this book: entrepreneurial leadership. This unique form of leadership is exhibited by individuals who seem to move mountains and joyfully engage others in that quest. It can extend to any industry or life pursuit. Additionally, it applies to entrepreneurs who start ventures from scratch, as well as leaders within large, established organizations.

What makes great entrepreneurial leaders like this? Why are we so drawn to them? To what extent do we each have this kind of talent within us? Can it be honed and drawn out more to help us accomplish our goals? These are the questions that this book will help you to answer.

So, let's start with a simple related question worth asking: Is this something you are born with, or is it something you can learn and hone? I believe the answer to this nature-versus-nurture argument in this case is that it's a bit of both. I believe that one can be born with some of this talent, and I also believe that it can be learned and developed. So, let's kick off the story there with a bit about child's play. I'll loosely follow the five-act structure of a play as I did in *Self Less*, and it begins with a fun tale about pirates on the high seas.

ACT ONE

CHILD'S PLAY

I CAN'T STAND to be bored. I figured that out very early on as a kid growing up in the San Francisco Bay Area. I was totally bored out of my mind sitting around the house reading comic books or watching cartoons on television. I was happiest when playing actively and creatively, preferably outside. At those moments, I would get into what my former Claremont Graduate University (CGU) colleague Mihaly "Mike" Csikszentmihalyi (1990) called "flow," totally lost in whatever I was imagining and/or building.

My younger brother Steve and I loved to build forts out in the backyard and, on rainy days, in the house using furniture, blankets, and pillows. Our outside forts became home turfs that were protected in battle, and our indoor forts often became imagined sailing vessels on long and treacherous voyages.

I remember one rainy Bay Area afternoon when a storm left things too wet outside for us to build a fort out in the backyard. Instead, we decided to build a fort inside our family room. My mom allowed us to move all the furniture to the middle of the room, all nestled together on top of the center of a large rug. She then let us roll up the edges of the rug into the shape of a ship, with all the furniture creating areas of the ship for my brother and me to sit on and climb into.

To us, the structure resembled a mighty vessel we were piloting on some grand adventure. Out at the edges of the room, any bare floor outside the rug was shark infested and not to be touched. We were pirates on the high seas, and I do remember some pirate-style singing, swashbuckling, falling overboard, and being saved, and there might have been some makeshift swords involved and perhaps a bandana or two in use. Best of all, my mom played along and served us lunch on the boat, careful to avoid the treacherous waters surrounding our vessel.

As I reflect on my early days and memories like this, I can't emphasize enough the importance of creative play for children (Ginsburg 2007; Singer et al. 2006). My colleagues in early childhood development assert that children who are encouraged and assisted in creative play during their formative years not only develop their creative thinking in enjoyable ways but also gain general cognitive capabilities, along with strong contextual problem-solving skills (Russ 2016). In creative play, kids must pay attention, understand how things work, and analyze why they work, all in service of a scenario or scene in their minds. In my case, we also actively interacted with and commandeered elements in our immediate environment toward a specific purpose.

I would also add that my mom's encouragement meant a lot. Just having her acknowledge and support our creative play showed us that it was not only acceptable but also encouraged. It also meant a lot to play in this way with my younger brother, and so, social skills were being developed, negotiated, and adjudicated. Who would play what role, and who would be the first to walk the plank and be saved?

CREATE MORE LESSON:

Creative play at an early age is critical to developing as an entrepreneurial leader.

I think that creative play is particularly important in the development of an entrepreneurial leader. To make this point, let me extend my story to the fun things we did as we grew out of our adventures on the high seas. As we got a little older, creative play happened less and less. We got more and more involved in typical pursuits for growing boys, such as pick-up baseball games (more on baseball later), but we also found that we really liked to build things.

We built coasters, bikes, and skateboards and jumped our bikes over homemade ramps out in front of our house. It probably didn't hurt that our dad and our older brother were continually tinkering with and building antique cars and hot rods. I can't help but think that all of that, including our early adventures in building extravagant and creative forts, laid the foundation for the other things we built as we got older.

My mom helped us open savings accounts very early on and taught us well about saving and using money. She then encouraged us to go out and make money as well. As soon as we were allowed to, my brother and I would canvas the neighborhood, cutting lawns, trimming trees, and doing just about anything to make an extra buck to spend down at the local 7-Eleven or on our bike and skateboard upgrades. I think that this was an integral part of our entrepreneurial training: learning the value of money and saving. Even more to the point, we were learning how to generate our own income at a very early age.

Think about some of these key building blocks. Creative play, building things, and later, generating a little commerce in our neighborhood were all combined in a special way to help plant the early seeds of entrepreneurship, all encouraged by my mom. Our actual first foray in entrepreneurship, selling our yard services in the neighborhood, would eventually integrate very well with all the encouragement and support we had gotten from my mom to build forts, coasters, bikes, skateboards, LEGO structures, model cars, little Pinewood Derby cars, and grand vessels set for the high seas. Whether we're talking about fort-building or launching a start-up, the roots often trace back to those early experiences when we learned to build, adapt, and try things our own way.

Young Entrepreneurs as Builders

In my latter years of high school, our mom really leaned in and indulged our entrepreneurial drive and our desire to hone our skills with our skateboards. We wanted to design and build a full-size skateboard half-pipe to satisfy our growing interest in the sport. We began with a very detailed scale model in our shop class under the direction of our great shop teacher, John.

With John's help, we then used that scale model to construct a large skating half-pipe that was more than eight feet wide, more than ten feet high, and about twenty feet in length. It was so impressive that our local newspaper ran a story on it, complete with pictures of my brother and me flinging ourselves nearly out of the structure and into thin air. We also went to great lengths to find a heavy-duty truck and flatbed trailer to transport our creations from school to our house. My mom was there, encouraging us every step of the way, and she very generously made up the difference for the remaining amount we couldn't pay for from our side jobs. She was our angel investor in more ways than one.

I don't mean to leave out my dad, as we learned a lot from him as well. I think that the primary quality we learned from him that is relevant to entrepreneurial leadership was his work ethic. My dad worked hard as a fireman in San Francisco, and, as did many firefighters at the time, he always had some sort of side job or small business venture going in his off-hours.

We got to see him work hard and tirelessly, pretty much twenty-four hours a day, and we saw how this enabled him to provide for our family. So while my mom provided supportive early training, my dad provided a powerful role model. Indeed, we come from a long line of small businesspeople in our Italian family. Small businesses and hard work were in our DNA, going back generations.

Prompted by that background, as my brother and I moved through high school, we eagerly took on odd jobs here and there. Working hard and earning money were very important to us both. Soon after high school, I worked a part-time job while going to school as an undergraduate college student, and I would return home to Fort Jones, California, to take on full-time summer jobs to help pay my way through college.

These were typically low-level, low-paying jobs that involved repetitive and routine tasks and physically hard work. I happily worked these jobs to make money for college, but the jobs were often so repetitive and routine that they were mentally excruciating for me to perform. I couldn't stand doing work like that, and it influenced my future in ways I could not have predicted.

Some of the summer jobs, such as tending cattle, cutting alfalfa, and fighting forest fires, were exhilarating at times, but they clearly weren't things I wanted to be doing for the rest of my life. Other jobs, including stocking shelves at the market, cleaning up at the bowling alley at night, and changing out sprinkler pipes in the fields, were so mindless and boring that a short time in each job would drive me nuts.

I couldn't wait to get those summer jobs over with and go back to college to be stimulated in class and working toward something bigger. While I hadn't yet heard the adage "If you love what you do, you'll never work a day in your life," it fit so well with how I felt about work and its role in my life. In fact, one summer job really hit the mark for me. I found it after I had finished my undergrad degree and was getting ready for grad school. Best of all, it was something I created from scratch and was so proud of.

I had just wrapped up my undergrad degree that spring and had enrolled in an MBA program for the fall. I loved school and did not want to waste any time, so I went straight from my undergrad course into that MBA program. I was looking for something fun and stimulating to do for that summer back home, but I could not find anything that was suitable. Feeling desperate that I hadn't lined anything up, I walked into the regional hospital nearby and asked to meet with the CEO.

He wasn't available, but his executive assistant agreed to meet with me. I made the case that because they had had some negative and largely unwarranted press recently, they needed me to help them create a public relations and marketing capability at the hospital and work hard on rebuilding their image in the community. That took a lot of guts, but I was swinging for the fences on that one.

The executive assistant was intrigued and asked how I would do that, how much I would want to be paid, and how much of it I thought I could accomplish that summer before returning to college. She must have liked what I said because she said she would talk to the CEO about it and get back to me. Within a few days, she asked me to go back in and meet with her and the CEO and answer some questions.

We met soon after and did just that, and I was hired on the spot. Over the course of that summer, we not only did a lot of good for that hospital in rebuilding its brand in the community, but I also learned a valuable personal lesson: Sometimes, you've got to create opportunities for yourself. In addition, I learned that summer that I really liked working on something novel, complicated, and challenging.

CREATE MORE LESSON:

Sometimes, you must create opportunities for yourself.

It was starting to come together for me. As I described in *Self Less*, I loved my experience in the MBA program, learning so much from so many great professors in a lot of different areas and how to integrate it. It is important to be able to quickly size up any organization and figure out how to fix it or how to create a solution if one doesn't exist to serve a need. All of these invaluable teachings really opened my mind to what I could accomplish. In that program, I filled in some important gaps in my thinking, namely how business works, what works well and what doesn't, why so many businesses fail, what makes great companies successful, and how to launch a business.

Once again, I needed a summer job to squeeze in between the first and second years of my MBA program. I worked with some family friends and landed a summer job as a sales engineer for a start-up—a membrane circuit manufacturer in Phoenix, Arizona. While stressful at times, it was a lot of fun and really opened my eyes. I admired the engineers we worked with, as well as the founder and main investor. These were actual tech entrepreneurs whom I admired very much, and I wondered how I could do what they were doing someday.

Both that early summer internship helping the hospital rethink and rebrand and that exposure to real tech entrepreneurs the following summer served me well as I neared the completion of my MBA. Coming out of the MBA program, I interviewed for full-time jobs and received a couple of good offers from two very well-known companies with national brands. The trouble was that with both of those corporate jobs, the work seemed so incredibly boring.

The work just wasn't at all appealing to me and seemed to be totally easy and repetitive. Based on my prior experience, I knew that either of those jobs would have driven me nuts within months, if not weeks. In fact, I felt that I had accomplished more in the summer internship at the local hospital than I ever would in the corporate jobs being offered to me. I wasn't sure what to do, but I knew that I didn't want to do either of those jobs.

I explained all of this to my MBA program advisor, Bernie, who turned out to be an invaluable lifelong mentor to me. He asked if I would consider pursuing a PhD in business, and my honest reply was, "Wow, what's a PhD? And what do you do with it?" I really hadn't thought about continuing in college, and I didn't understand what a doctorate entailed. I needed help.

Bernie gave me a crash course on what a doctoral program was and what you could do with your doctorate. It was all so intriguing to me. Working as a faculty member sounded very interesting, particularly because it would enable me to learn continually throughout my life by conducting research on topics of my choosing and teaching new subjects. That would certainly check off the boredom box for me. Bernie helped me apply to and eventually get into the doctoral program in business at the University of Arizona. His help was so influential in my life and my new pursuit of the *life of the mind.* He was hard on me at times, but he is right up there on my personal Mount Rushmore of the greats.

Ironically, although I had all this entrepreneurial training that could lead me to start my own company, I decided to keep going to college. I entered the PhD program at the University of Arizona, which had just become an Association of American Universities (AAU) institution (one of the topflight research universities across the country). I studied at the business school and majored in organizational behavior (OB) in the Department of Management. I also chose to minor in MIS in the Department of Management Information Systems. It was exactly the right combination, as information technology and its adoption by organizations were exploding in growth and types of applications. I could see that the doctoral program was going to open many different opportunities and directions for me.

With my business experience and training at that point, and the fact that I had loved it all so much, it seemed natural to continue my doctoral studies at a business school. Next, given that I really excelled in and loved my undergrad and MBA courses that had to do with people and how they act and think, choosing to major in OB was a perfect fit. Essentially the study of human behavior in organizational settings, OB includes topics such as leadership, team building, goal setting, and even macro topics (for instance, organizational strategy and structure), as well as my personal favorites—innovation and entrepreneurship.

I knew that the OB major was the right choice for me, but I was a little worried that it might be too theoretical and that I might need to complement that major with a minor area of study that was a bit more applied and practical. I did research on a bunch of potential areas of study, and I kept coming back to computers. I really enjoyed my prior computer-related courses, and in my previous work experience, I liked doing some light programming and installing personal computers and printers in offices and labs.

Indeed, the personal computer and local area networking revolution was just kicking into high gear, and an early version (BITNET) of the modern-day internet was just getting started. Given all of that, the decision as to what to minor in was easy. This was why I opted to minor in MIS. I was lucky that the business school in Arizona had a top-ranked MIS department literally right next door to the Department of Management.

The PhD Really Worked Out for Me

Call it good decision-making or just plain good luck, but those choices worked out well for me. I concluded my doctorate by working on a dissertation aimed at the nexus of personal computing, local area networks, and a new thing called groupware that enabled people to collaborate with each other on their desktop computers. This was all pre-internet, and local area networks were brand new.

A senior professor in the MIS department, Jay, had built a lab there with the help of other faculty members and a bunch of doctoral students like me. The lab included networked PCs all around a custom conference table. More importantly, software applications had been written that enabled teams to use the PCs in that facility and work together to do things such as generate ideas, reflect on each other's ideas, rank the ideas, decide on a course of action, flesh out an action plan, and so on, all in real time. This was essentially the early precursor to today's internet-based social media platforms, such as Facebook and X (formerly Twitter), or collaboration platforms, including Google Workspace, Microsoft Teams, and Zoom. It was amazing and so far ahead of its time, and I couldn't wait to figure out how to get involved.

Up till then, Jay and his team were doing what we called design science, focused primarily on building out the software, perfecting the architecture of the network and facility, getting feedback from business groups that paid to come in and use the facility, and making improvements to the software and other elements based on feedback from the user groups. They were so busy in a very practical and iterative process of designing, building, securing feedback, redesigning, rebuilding, and so on that there just wasn't much time for them to investigate the social science behind the use of these applications and to develop and test social psychology theories of why and how people would adopt and adapt the technology.

I had studied a great deal about the relevant social science in my OB major area and had also learned psychological and social psychological research techniques in lab experimentation with human subjects. It made complete sense for me to take all my newly gained knowledge and experience from OB and apply them to what I was seeing in this incredible new computer lab. I wasn't the only one at the business school who figured this out, as a couple of other doctoral students jumped into this nexus with me.

One in particular (Joe, my charismatic colleague with whom I joined WSU) was a very close friend and fellow doctoral student who was majoring in MIS and minoring in the Department of Management—the opposite of what I was doing. He and I worked very closely on these early lab experiments and related published articles, and he went on to publish some of the most seminal work in this new field.

Joe and I were later asked to document this early work together in a 2019 article in the *Journal of Information Systems Education* (Jessup and Valacich 2019). Suffice it to say, in the words of Kuhn (1997) in his seminal work, *The Structure of Scientific Revolutions*, we got in early and rode the wave of foundational, basic research on the use of collaboration technologies. We were very lucky to be there together at the right time in the right place.

I tell these stories about my experiences in the MBA program and the PhD program, not so much to say that everything else beforehand prepared me for these grad school experiences. Indeed, all the early creative play, experience in building things, training in generating and managing money, growing up with entrepreneurs, and performing jobs that were sheer drudgery versus jobs that were fun and entrepreneurial shaped me in important ways that enabled me to excel in grad school and leverage the heck out of it (Dickel et al. 2021). The important point, however, is not so much what I brought to grad school but what grad school gave me to take into the rest of my life.

How Does College Help Entrepreneurial Leaders?

The most important entrepreneurial life lesson for me from all of grad school can be summed up in one word: *aperture*. Think of the aperture of a camera, opening and closing to allow more or less light into your view, which affects the images you see and the depth of field available to you. Much like a camera, we each have an aperture in our mind's eye that either constrains or enables what we see in life. More importantly, our aperture plays a huge role in what we see as being open and available to us, making it possible for us to achieve or even attempt things (Krueger 2007).

For a moment, think about me as a high school athlete heading down to the College of the Siskiyous to play baseball. I went in thinking that I would just play ball and that would be the end of it, but I learned that I could gain a business certificate and go back home and get a decent administrative job in one of the many businesses or municipal agencies back home. Better yet, I learned that I could get much of my general education requirements finished and out of the way and then leverage that by attending a university to earn a four-year degree. Going in, my aperture didn't include attaining a degree, but on the way out, that was now a possibility for me. My aperture expanded.

Similarly, going into my undergrad course, I thought that my primary option afterward was to get a sales-oriented job down in Sacramento or up in Medford, Oregon. On the way out, I realized that I could work in several good business jobs throughout the Western United States. I also learned that I could get an MBA, a degree I hadn't even heard of before. After my undergrad studies, my aperture widened again. Same story for the MBA program.

On the way in, I thought my option would be one of the better jobs regionally, but on the way out, I found that I could get one of many good business jobs not only in the Bay Area but also in other hot markets at the time, including Southern California and Texas. Best of all, I learned that I could earn a PhD, another degree that I'd had no clue about. My aperture widened yet again.

Next, I went into the doctoral program in Arizona, thinking I could go back to either Chico State or nearby Sacramento State and be a professor. In this program, I learned about the life of the mind, how cutting-edge, world-class research is conducted, and the burgeoning field of collaboration technologies, and I realized I could be a faculty member anywhere in the world. I also learned that I could go into management consulting, I could be a research scientist at a company such as Microsoft, or I could start a company based on my experience in the lab. My aperture was so wide that it included nearly everything. All was possible and available to me at that point.

CREATE MORE LESSON:

Our aperture in life, perhaps more than anything, determines our destiny.

I suppose that is one of the things I've loved most about higher education: It has given me the opportunity to help widen the aperture for students. Exposing them to new experiences expands their ways of thinking, allowing them to view new things from different perspectives and literally broadening their horizons and thoughts about what is possible for them. I've been able to do this for countless students, both undergraduates and graduate students, and it is perhaps the most rewarding part of a career in higher education.

I remember one recent grad student in particular, who came in thinking he would earn a doctorate in public health and then go work for the local county health department—a noble pursuit indeed. While with us, he decided to earn an MBA and then figured out that he could combine his public health and business training in interesting ways.

Consequently, on the way out, he realized he could also be a faculty member anywhere, work at the state or federal level as a public health expert or work in industry, go into consulting, or start a company based on his knowledge and experience. His aperture opened significantly and at just the right time as we were coming out of the pandemic. His sense of what was possible grew tremendously.

This aperture effect is so powerful that, at my last institution, we implemented what we called the time capsule project, through which we captured new, incoming grad students' thoughts about their intentions after getting their degrees. We then revisited these students later, as they neared graduation, to measure again their sense of what they perceived to be available to them. This enabled us to gauge the extent to which there had been a change in their beliefs about their opportunities from their entry into graduate school to their exit from graduate school. We aimed to literally measure changes in their apertures. My team began collecting these data just before I retired, and I anxiously await their findings.

Key Elements in Developing as an Entrepreneurial Leader

Some people think entrepreneurs are born with a certain mindset, but I've seen firsthand that it can be developed. Researchers define the entrepreneurial mindset as a way of thinking that encompasses recognizing opportunities, persisting through ambiguity, and acting with initiative—even when the path is unclear (Neck et al. 2025). When students start to see problems as chances to build something new, that's the entrepreneurial mindset at work. And once that switch flips, it can shape how they think for the rest of their lives.

So, let's think about what I've addressed so far. I feel that many elements from my life have contributed directly to my entrepreneurial leadership capabilities. We discussed the role of creative play at an early age, as well as the importance of encouragement and support in building things. We covered training in making and managing money, particularly through simple entrepreneurial ventures during childhood. We emphasized learning from entrepreneurial role models early on, along with working with and gaining insights from actual entrepreneurs as young adults. We highlighted the value of exploring various types of jobs to better identify which roles and tasks one genuinely loves. Finally, we explored experiences such as attending graduate school and how they can broaden one's perspective on what is possible.

All of these are incredibly helpful. Even better, they aren't the only pathways to becoming an entrepreneurial leader. There are also great programs offered in high school, such as the Distributive Education Clubs of America (DECA), founded in 1946, which help to train and hone budding entrepreneurs. Many communities offer founder meetups, networking events, pitch competitions, and other related programming that is extremely beneficial. Nearby universities and municipalities sometimes offer formal business plan competitions, and those are very helpful as well. Universities also often offer full-blown entrepreneurship majors to undergrads (and even grad students), and those are widespread and very popular now. Some universities even offer neat live and learn entrepreneurial experiences on campus, such as the Lassonde Entrepreneur Institute at the University of Utah.

My point here is, there are all kinds of ways to develop your entrepreneurial leadership capabilities all around the country and the world right now. For older adults, there is also some great executive education programming, both in person and online, on entrepreneurship available from leading business schools all across the country. The good news is that you've got lots of options.

I certainly had options, thank goodness. All that entrepreneurial training and preparation paid off handsomely. They found their way into my DNA, you might say. Even today, well into my sixties, if given a choice, I would much rather do something new and different rather than just continue to do what others have already done. Similarly, if forced to walk down the path that others have already taken, I would much rather do it in a new and different way. I would rather take the path less traveled, as Robert Frost said.

So, let's see where this path leads. Up until now, I've mostly talked about the role of training and experience in developing an entrepreneurial mindset. Next, let's explore entrepreneurial leadership in action, both in launching new things and, perhaps most importantly, working within mature organizations.

The important question here is not just Can I launch a start-up and make my dreams a reality? It's Can I be an entrepreneurial leader within my existing role inside my current organization? In short, Can I be an entrepreneurial leader at work?

ACT TWO

INNOVATING AT WORK

ENTREPRENEURSHIP HAS LONG been a hallmark of the US economy and ethos, and it is alive and well. For example, the US Census Bureau (2025) reported that in January 2025 alone, 392,496 business applications were filed in the US. Similarly, American Express announced that between January 2021 and December 2023, entrepreneurs filed 5.2 million "likely employer" business applications, a 34 percent increase compared to the 2017–2019 period (Baird and Heden 2024).

While many entrepreneurs are chasing the dream in the US, the start-up survival rates are not very good. Approximately 10 percent of start-ups fail within the first year. By the fifth year, nearly 50 percent of start-ups cease operations. Further, only about 35 percent of businesses remain operational by their tenth year (Punjwani 2024). Interestingly, the *New York Post* (2024) reported that a third of Americans identify as entrepreneurs, with millennials (39 percent) and Gen Z (36 percent) leading the way, compared to Gen X (29 percent) and baby boomers (25 percent). Entrepreneurship rates also surged by

18 percent for women and 20 percent for men in 2022, reaching all-time highs.

Investment in start-ups continues to be brisk. For example, in 2024, global venture funding totaled $66.5 billion in the third quarter alone (Teare 2024). *The Wall Street Journal* stated that median early-stage valuations for US companies reached a record high of $44.8 million in the same year, driven by investments in hot sectors, such as artificial intelligence (AI) (Chernova 2024). Dealroom data show that the value of start-ups in Las Vegas alone in 2024 was $19 billion, which I found to be staggering (privately sourced from https://dealroom.co). In terms of the economic significance of these small businesses, their value goes well beyond the impact of their innovative new products and services.

In 2024, the US Small Business Administration (2024) reported that small businesses accounted for a recent net increase of 2.6 million jobs, representing 80 percent of the total net job increase. In total, the US was home to approximately one million start-ups, employing around five million people, which constituted about 4 percent of the total private sector workforce, according to Clearly Payments (2024).

A scan of recent headlines on entrepreneurs and start-ups shows some interesting trends as well. For example, a *New York Post* (2024) article disclosed that Gen Zers are more likely than their parents or grandparents to be entrepreneurs. A Reuters article reported that US small businesses have recently surged, and sentiments about/from them have improved. Perhaps even more interestingly, an article in *The Guardian* (Marks 2024) mentioned that boomers are selling their businesses to millennials in a generational handover. These statistics and trends highlight the dynamic and evolving landscape of entrepreneurship and start-ups in the US, reflecting both the opportunities and challenges faced by new and existing businesses.

Do I Have to Be a Founder to Be an Entrepreneur?

When we think about entrepreneurs, we naturally think of the founders of start-ups—the pioneers whose activities those preceding paragraphs reported on. They are the courageous people who are willing to risk it all to chase their dreams and launch their companies. They are not, however, the only entrepreneurs worth talking about, and launching a start-up is not the only way to be entrepreneurial. All of us can be entrepreneurs in our lives and our work. All it takes is an entrepreneurial mindset, and you can apply it to just about anything to do or seek.

Earlier, I discussed developing an entrepreneurial mindset from early childhood through young adulthood, including graduate school. Those lessons and experiences have stuck with me and have carried through into my adult working life after graduate school. Don't get me wrong; I was fortunate enough to participate in some substantial entrepreneurial ventures along the way, including noteworthy wins and losses. In addition to helping hundreds of student ventures form and operate through our business plan competition at WSU, I've also been directly involved in many start-ups. Consider the examples below, along with my perspective on how they performed from a baseball standpoint.

- **Edge Up Learning:** Soon after earning my PhD, I developed an award-winning software prototype of a language learning game together with my former wife, and we won a Zenith Data Systems Masters of Innovation Award that year (1991). We toyed with the idea of creating a company around the game, but I was not fully ready to commit to the start-up, quit my faculty gig, and take a risk on the business. *Baseball box score: I didn't even step up to the plate.*

- **Patent Rank:** One of the brightest people I know is a former doctoral student who developed an incredible method to assess the value of a patent and rank it among a list of other patents using network analysis within the full US patent database. It was a fantastic idea, and he earned some decent money from his invention. I tried to assist him as a mentor and connector, but I didn't know enough at the time to help him gain the traction that he believed I could facilitate. *Baseball box score: Some foul balls and an occasional base hit.*

- **University Funds:** While I was running the entrepreneurship program at WSU, some alumni who were on my advisory board needed help launching a venture capital fund aimed at intellectual property emerging from universities across the country. They asked me to provide advisory and prep work for them, and I agreed. I toured the country, visiting tech transfer offices at dozens of major research universities, as well as a few national labs. I secured signed memorandum of agreement with nearly all of them, outlining how they would collaborate with the fund. It was a promising idea, but it came at the wrong time. Just as the founders were ready to begin raising funds, the Great Recession struck in 2007, and all investments dried up completely. *Baseball box score: The game was rained out and canceled.*

- **Xecutive Advisory Partners (XAP):** During the University Funds experience, I met a few guys with whom I liked to work, and we decided to create XAP together two years later. XAP is a boutique venture capital firm and business accelerator based in Seattle, Washington. XAP has been in operation for approximately fifteen years, and it has added a lot of value to start-ups all over the world, either in launching, growing, exiting, or getting unstuck. We've even participated in a few nice exits along the way. *Baseball box score: Several base hits and doubles, and a solid triple as well.*

- **Assaya and LiquaCool:** I helped form, launch, and secure seed funding for these two start-ups. Assaya is working to democratize health diagnostics with a state-of-the-art machine reader for lateral flow assay test strips (together with other innovative technologies). LiquaCool has come up with a clever way to cool overheated microprocessors. I serve on the boards of both companies and am having a blast helping them grow. *Baseball box score: A promising start in the very early innings.*
- **Desert Forge Ventures:** This is a newly launched venture capital fund focused on early-stage ventures in the Las Vegas valley. Our goal is to support the growth of outstanding tech and biotech companies that remain here in the valley, further developing and diversifying the local economy. I am the managing partner, and I've brought together an incredible team of venture partners, analysts, interns, investors, banking and corporate partners, advisors, and mentors. *Baseball box score: Swinging for the fence.*

Moreover, I sit on the boards of two very successful family businesses that one would call medium-size corporations, and I am also on the boards of and/or am informally advising several other new start-ups. Additionally, I serve as a fellow at the Lincy Institute at the University of Nevada, Las Vegas (UNLV), a public policy think tank. My first project with Lincy is a study of the entrepreneurial ecosystem in Las Vegas, and I have also been advising UNLV on the launch of a venture capital fund aimed at inventions coming out of UNLV (which led to the launch of Desert Forge Ventures). Therefore, when I say that I have dabbled in the start-up world and continue to do so, I'm doing a heck of a lot of dabbling!

The point here, however, is that you can dabble without being a full-time entrepreneur or even launching a start-up in the classic sense. You can be involved in the start-up scene the way I have done above. You can be entrepreneurial within large existing organizations as well.

In fact, we've seen some incredible entrepreneurial leaders in vast, complex corporations and other types of mature organizations. Several CEOs have demonstrated remarkable entrepreneurial leadership within large established corporations, effectively acting as *intrapreneurs*—driving innovation, transforming business models, and steering their companies to new frontiers. Research shows that intrapreneurs share the same mindset as founders: They're creative, strategic, and willing to take smart risks in the face of resistance (Neessen et al. 2019). But they also have to be savvy about organizational culture, politics, and timing. That makes their work even more impressive. They're not seeking permission—they're quietly reshaping what's possible.

Back at the beginning of this story, I discussed Steve Jobs at Apple as an example of an exceptional founder who returned to his large, complex company and saved it. He reinvented Apple from a struggling computer company into a global powerhouse with products such as the iMac, iPod, iPhone, and iPad.

Many other tech CEOs also fall into that category of successful intrapreneurs. Jeff Bezos founded Amazon, but his entrepreneurial mindset within the company as it has grown has been remarkable.

He has constantly disrupted industries (e.g., with Amazon Web Services, Amazon Prime, and Amazon Alexa) and has reinvented Amazon multiple times beyond e-commerce. Similarly, Elon Musk wasn't the founder of Tesla. He took over as CEO and turned it into an innovation-driven juggernaut.

Musk applied an entrepreneurial, risk-taking approach to scale Tesla from a niche start-up to a global leader in electric vehicles (EVs). Satya Nadella took over Microsoft in 2014 and transformed it from a stagnating tech giant into a cloud-first company. His leadership in pushing Microsoft Azure, AI, and cloud computing made Microsoft one of the most valuable companies in the world. Tim Cook at Apple? Same story. Reed Hastings at Netflix fits this mold as well, as does Ginni Rometty at IBM.

And it's not just at these tech giants where you find great intrapreneurship. For example, Bob Iger led Disney's transformation by acquiring Pixar, Marvel, Lucasfilm (*Star Wars*), and 21st Century Fox, turning Disney into an unrivaled content empire. He also launched Disney+, positioning the company in the streaming wars. Mary Barra took over General Motors and aggressively pushed the company toward EVs, autonomous cars, and sustainability, revamping a legacy automaker into a forward-thinking, tech-driven company.

Similarly, Indra Nooyi led PepsiCo's transition from a junk food–focused company into a healthier, sustainability-driven business. She expanded the company's portfolio to include healthier foods and beverages while growing global market share. These leaders share a common trait: They acted like entrepreneurs within their massive corporations, taking bold risks, disrupting industries, and driving massive transformations (Neessen et al. 2019).

Another great example here is Geisha Williams, former CEO of Pacific Gas & Electric Company (PG&E) and the first Latinx

CEO of a Fortune 500 company. Williams began her career as an engineering supervisor and rose through the ranks to lead one of the largest utility companies in the US. She spearheaded the transition to renewable energy, making PG&E the largest solar utility provider in the country under her leadership—an example of visionary transformation within a mature industry. Williams is a first-generation Cuban American whose path from immigrant daughter to CEO exemplifies personal resilience and purpose-driven leadership.

CREATE MORE LESSON:

Intrapreneurs take bold risks, disrupt industries, and drive massive transformations, much like entrepreneurs do.

As I reflect on my adult life and my career in higher education, I see that the early seeds of entrepreneurship have nicely carried over into my role as an intrapreneur in my professional life. For example, experiencing that innovative collaboration facility firsthand as a doctoral student in Arizona left a huge impression on me. I then went on to help build similar research labs at several other universities, and I also contributed to the design and construction of dozens of modern, state-of-the-art classrooms across many universities.

Even more to the point, that experience led me to help design and build at least three classroom-of-the-future facilities at WSU, the University of Arizona, and CGU. Back in Arizona as a doctoral student, my aperture was opened wide in terms of facilities. I saw what was possible, and it lit a flame. I went on to do many more similar labs and classrooms of numerous different varieties.

I can think of so many other examples in my work life in higher education in which I felt that I acted not only as an intrapreneur but also as a change agent. Some examples include

- helping to implement a first-in-the-country laptop requirement for students in the highly ranked MBA program at Indiana's Kelley School of Business and porting all the learning over to the Lotus Notes software platform;
- helping to design, build, and launch an online undergrad program in MIS at WSU well before anyone else anywhere was contemplating doing this;
- running the entrepreneurship program at WSU, developing a world-class business plan competition, and achieving a national ranking for the program;
- figuring out a way to continue the rankings trajectory for great programs within the Eller College of Management (my alma mater) at the University of Arizona while also helping that business school to become more of a self-sustaining entity on campus;
- quickly launching and funding a new medical school, constructing a world-class football stadium without the necessary resources, driving regional economic development, and helping to achieve Carnegie R1 research status for UNLV; and
- finding a way to help CGU, a nearly one-hundred-year-old private university, based primarily on small, intimate, face-to-face seminars, to shift boldly to online and hybrid learning and focus more on high-demand professional study areas.

As I mentioned in *Self Less*, I could probably put together a master class on leading these various organizational transformations. But for expediency, let's simply focus here on what it takes for a leader to successfully push these types of changes and innovations through an organization. Let's return to that base-level definition of entrepreneurial leadership that we began with and see how it applies to this notion of being an intrapreneur.

Intrapreneurs Are Indeed Entrepreneurs

We began this story by discussing what it takes to be an entrepreneurial leader. Creative visionaries are willing to take risks and are able to transform their vision into sound plans and then into action. They are also skilled at persuading others to follow them, either through words or by simply setting an example, driven by a strong desire to see their vision come to fruition and possessing the resilience to persevere in the face of significant adversity (Antonakis and Autio 2007). This same definition applies whether we are talking about an entrepreneur launching a start-up or an intrapreneur leading their team or organization through substantial organizational change.

Let's examine each of these essential elements for being an entrepreneurial leader and apply them to a leader within an existing organization, who is aiming to guide their team or organization through significant changes. Here we go!

Creativity: First, in addition to base-level intelligence and capability, intrapreneurs also need to be creative and visionary, just like start-up entrepreneurs. They need to be creative in the sense that they must be able to think outside the box and not be weighed down by the status quo within the organization (Neessen et al. 2019). They are not mired down in bureaucracy and old ways of doing things. They might, alternatively, be aware of what other companies are doing in other industries, recognizing the best practices and seeing that they are applicable and of value to their immediate team or organization.

Vision—Intrapreneurs also need to have vision in the sense that they need to be able to see what is possible for the team and the organization. What might the future look like, and how will the changes bring the team or organization closer to that bright future (Rigtering and Weitzel 2013)? Perhaps the immediate team or organization can focus more on the clients' needs, for example. Maybe the team just needs to listen to the clients more, value their input, put that learning into action, implement it, and really buy into strong client analytics. Then, the team or organization might become a client-centric leader within the industry at a very high level. That's a great vision for the company.

Risk-taking: Like a start-up entrepreneur, an intrapreneur must also be willing to take risks, jettisoning old, tired ways of doing things and being willing to try something new with the team or organization (Antoncic and Hisrich 2003). Sure, it might not work, but they see that something must be done, and the chances of failure are greater if nothing at all is done. To take some of the risk out, the intrapreneur in our example above might obtain industry benchmarks for a more client-centric approach to make sure that any changes are guided by experience. Similarly, the intrapreneur might first experiment with a small group of clients before implementing the approach across all clients.

Charisma: The intrapreneur must also be able to persuade others convincingly that their vision is the right one and that their plan of action is believable and will work (Antonakis et al. 2016; Neessen et al. 2019). The same charisma and skills of persuasion that successful entrepreneurs have are also very applicable to intrapreneurs. One could argue that these skills might even be more important, given that organizations might have a thick organizational culture and calcification around certain ways of doing things. In our example, the intrapreneur might use the benchmark evidence as the basis for a solid argument for the need for the change to a more client-centric approach. They might also employ narrative storytelling based on specific examples with key clients to help persuade others about the need for change.

Drive: The intrapreneur must also have that same intense drive to see their vision come to fruition. Moving a mature organization from point A to point B isn't easy, and intrapreneurs must fundamentally believe in what they are doing and have immense motivation and energy to carry it out (Neessen et al. 2019). They must wake up in the morning excited and focused on getting the job done. It won't be easy persuading others in the team or organization to change, so the intrapreneurs' drive and strong will are going to be paramount here as well.

Resilience: Similarly, intrapreneurs must have resilience to continue in the face of strong adversity and outright opposition. They must be willing to keep going despite resistance, both visible and not so easy to see (e.g., passive-aggressive behavior). The intrapreneur might, for example, encounter team members who are opposed to the shift in client approach. They might choose to meet them head-on and sit down with them to try to better understand and learn from their trepidation about this change. They might also have to spend extra time countering any misinformation being spread around the organization regarding the change. They'll have to persevere in the face of what might be intense pushback (Haynie et al. 2010).

You can see that the same elements of the definition of entrepreneurial leadership apply whether we are talking about an entrepreneur launching a start-up or an intrapreneur about to lead their team or organization through a significant organizational change. Now, some might argue that it's still a little different for the intrapreneur. They don't have to sell anything like an entrepreneur does, right?

I would tend to disagree, especially if they are trying to convince others within their organization about a change that includes the company's product and/or service line. Even if it doesn't, that intrapreneur still has to sell a new idea and a new way of doing things, and getting people to buy into that can be just as difficult as getting people to buy a start-up's new offerings.

Similarly, some might argue that for the intrapreneur, it's different because they must have built-in respect from people within the organization before these people follow them on this new path. That respect might come from their title, authority, qualifications, achievements, experience, and several other sources. It all adds up in a way that tells people within the organization, "Wow, this person knows what they are talking about. I believe them, and we should follow them." Is that really any different from the entrepreneur selling their new wares? Do we believe in their credibility less?

Some might say that the intrapreneur needs to be savvier organizationally than an entrepreneur, able to read the tea leaves of organizational politics, and able to understand people within the organization and their motivations, aspirations, allies, enemies, and so on. Again, is that really any different from the emotional intelligence that an entrepreneur must have to be successful in dealing with consumers, competitors, partners, regulators, investors, and team members?

CREATE MORE LESSON:

Intrapreneurs must persuade, sell, be credible, and be savvy, much like entrepreneurs.

You can see that many of the qualities of the entrepreneur readily apply to the intrapreneur as well. There has been a good deal of discussion and research on the differences between the two types of leaders, but I really think that they are much more alike than they are different. Intrapreneurs are simply entrepreneurs operating within existing organizations (Antoncic and Hisrich 2003). In fact, I believe that we can all draw from the entrepreneurial world to be even better agents of change within our organizations.

To make that point, let's look at some specific concepts and techniques that entrepreneurs typically use and apply them to intrapreneurship. There are many aspects of launching and growing start-ups that apply to organizational change. Here are some examples that help make my point.

Entrepreneur Best Practices Applied to Intrapreneurs

OK, so now let's look at some of the best practices from the entrepreneurship world and see how they apply to intrapreneurs taking on big changes inside mature organizations. These change agents can benefit from many of the tools and techniques that founders frequently use. Let's start with the notion of a minimal viable product (MVP).

Minimal viable product: For entrepreneurs, an MVP is the simplest version of a product that includes just enough features to satisfy early customers and gather feedback for future development (Lenarduzzi and Taibi 2016). The goal of an MVP is to 1) quickly test an idea using minimal resources, 2) validate market demand before making significant investments, and 3) collect real user feedback to enhance and refine the product.

For example, if you're a start-up launching a new app, instead of building a full-feature version, you might release a basic version with core functionality to see if users like it and want to use it. If they do, you iterate and improve. If not, you pivot or abandon the idea before wasting time and money. This same concept applies to the intrapreneur as well. Has your idea or initiative got enough behind it to launch and convince people to support it, or is it still half-baked and inviting doubt or criticism?

Unique value proposition (UVP): Let's try another concept from the entrepreneurial world. Entrepreneurs often strive for a UVP, a clear statement that explains what makes their new product, service, or company different and better than the competition (Majka 2024). It highlights the unique benefits they offer to their customers and why the customers should choose them over the alternatives. A strong UVP should clearly communicate the benefits to the customer, differentiate the product from those of the competitors, and be specific and easy to understand. This is no different for an intrapreneur. In fact, if people within the organization can't readily see how your new approach clearly adds value vis-à-vis an existing approach, it will be very difficult, if not impossible, to get people to go along with your new way of doing things.

Addressable, obtainable, and serviceable market: Another popular set of related concepts within the entrepreneurs' (and investors') tool kit comprises TAM, SAM, and SOM. These market-sizing concepts can also apply to leading change within an existing organization by helping leaders identify the scope and impact of their initiatives. Let's define each below and see how it might apply to intrapreneurs.

The total addressable market (TAM) is the entire potential market for a product, service, or change initiative. Within an existing organization, this might be the broadest group that could be affected by the change that is being considered (e.g., all employees if implementing a new leadership model). The serviceable available market (SAM) is the segment of TAM that your organization can realistically reach based on constraints such as geography, resources, or readiness. Within an existing organization, this might be a specific department or business unit that is within reach financially or geographically. The serviceable obtainable market (SOM) is the portion of SAM that can be captured or influenced in the short term. Within an existing organization, this is the initial group of more willing stakeholders who are perhaps most likely to adopt and champion the change (Glasser and Shay 2025).

Let's use an example to show how these might apply to a specific change within an existing organization: When launching a digital transformation within an organization, TAM would be all employees who could use the new tools. In the case of a budget and training limit rollout, SAM would be perhaps just the employees in a pilot group. If the change starts with some very early adopters, SOM might be the core team of champions who are driving the initiative. You can see how this framework helps leaders prioritize efforts, manage expectations, and scale change effectively within an organization.

Lean LaunchPad: Just to drive this point home that we can learn from entrepreneurs, I'll use another solid example and show how it helps intrapreneurs. The Lean LaunchPad methodology, developed by Steve Blank (2012), is a hands-on approach to launching start-ups, which focuses on rapid experimentation, customer discovery, and iterative learning. It adheres to the Lean Start-Up principles (Blank 2013) and emphasizes the following:

1. Business model canvas (BMC): Instead of writing a full business plan, start-ups map out their assumptions using the BMC, a one-page strategic tool.
2. Customer discovery: Founders get out of the building to test their assumptions, gather real feedback, and refine their ideas.
3. Build-measure-learn: Rather than launching a fully built product, start-ups create an MVP, test it with customers, gather data, and iterate quickly based on the feedback.
4. Pivot or persevere: If evidence shows the initial idea is flawed, the start-up either pivots (changes direction) or perseveres (continues improving).

This applies very nicely to the work of intrapreneurs and those driving innovation within existing organizations. They can use Lean LaunchPad to develop new initiatives, products, or processes with less risk and greater efficiency. Here's how:

1. Business model adaptation: Instead of creating an external-facing BMC, intrapreneurs can use a mission model canvas tailored for internal innovation.
2. Internal customer discovery: The intrapreneur identifies key stakeholders, departments, and employees who will use or be affected by the change. They get real-world feedback before committing resources.

3. Experimentation and MVPs: Intrapreneurs can test new ideas in small, controlled environments before scaling. This could be a pilot program, a prototype, or a policy change within a single business unit.
4. Data-driven decisions: The intrapreneur gathers metrics on engagement, adoption, and outcomes to determine whether to scale, refine, or abandon the initiative.
5. Fail fast, learn fast: Like start-ups, intrapreneurs should embrace an agile mindset—test assumptions, fail small, and iterate quickly rather than launching massive projects doomed to bureaucratic slowdowns.

Let's just say, for example, that an intrapreneur within a large corporation wants to introduce AI-powered customer service. In that situation, a Lean LaunchPad approach would start with a BMC outlining the value to customers and internal feasibility. Next, the intrapreneur might conduct an internal customer discovery with the employees handling support. The team might then develop a small-scale pilot using AI for FAQs. The team members can then gather data and iterate before committing to full-scale deployment. You can see how that sense of experimenting, failing fast, learning fast, and so on readily applies to the intrapreneur and can be incredibly helpful.

CREATE MORE LESSON:

Entrepreneurs' techniques and tools can be very helpful to intrapreneurs.

Design thinking: Let's grab one more concept that is helpful to intrapreneurs, and this one definitely very closely aligns with entrepreneurial thinking. Design thinking is a human-centered, iterative approach that helps people drive innovation within an organization by solving real problems efficiently (Brown 2009). The five key stages in design thinking apply nicely to the work of an intrapreneur:

1. Empathize: Understand internal stakeholders' needs, frustrations, and workflows.
2. Define: Clearly frame the problem based on real challenges.
3. Ideate: Brainstorm potential solutions with teams.
4. Prototype: Develop quick, low-cost versions of new processes, products, or policies.
5. Test: Gather feedback, refine, and iterate before full-scale implementation.

First, this can be helpful to the intrapreneur in that it might reduce resistance to change in the sense that solutions are built with employees, not imposed on them. Second, it might help drive efficiency in that it encourages quick testing of new ideas before committing major resources. Third, it encourages cross-team collaboration in that it can help break silos by engaging multiple departments. Finally, it aligns innovation with business goals in that it helps to ensure new ideas serve both employees and company objectives (Brown 2009).

Let's look at an example of intrapreneurship in which a corporate HR team uses design thinking to improve employee retention. The team might interview employees about workplace frustrations (empathize). Next, the team members might define the problem as "onboarding is overwhelming, leading to early turnover" (define). They might then brainstorm ideas, such as a mentorship program or simplified training (ideate). Afterward, they test a small-scale mentorship pilot (prototype). Finally, they gather feedback, refine, and expand the program (test and iterate). As Liedtka (2011) noted, this approach works especially well in complex organizations because it's collaborative, iterative, and deeply human-centered. It helps leaders build buy-in by involving stakeholders early and often—so change isn't something done to people, but with them. Design thinking is clearly a helpful tool for intrapreneurs, providing a more modern, human-centered alternative to prior models of organizational change, including business process reengineering or more statistically driven change processes, such as Six Sigma.

So to recap, we can see that the characteristics of successful entrepreneurs apply well to intrapreneurs. They share many characteristics, and both are valuable and important types of leaders. We can also learn much from the entrepreneurial world and apply it in helpful ways to the intrapreneurial world. Concepts such as MVP and UVP apply easily and are helpful to change agents within organizations. Further, other tools, including design thinking, are immensely helpful to those leading change in organizations. There are so many helpful tools and concepts at your disposal, whether you are an aspiring (or practicing) intrapreneur or entrepreneur. There is so much to help those of us who are working hard to innovate at work.

Next, let's think about one critical aspect of a successful entrepreneurial leader—the leader's mindset. I'm going to break that down into two parts: ethos and persona. How do the leaders think about themselves, and, in turn, how do team members think about the leader?

Equally important, who is the leader deep down inside, and what drives them? And how is their mindset different from that of an ordinary leader? Finally, how does that mindset enable a transformational leader, one who can not only lead incredible teams to huge achievements but can also cause their team members to undergo incredible personal transformation in the process (Bass and Riggio 2006)?

ACT THREE

THE TRANSFORMATIONAL LEADER

GREAT LEADERS, WHETHER entrepreneurs or intrapreneurs, are what James MacGregor Burns (2003) called transformational leaders. Burns contrasted transactional leadership (focused on exchanges and short-term goals) with transformational leadership, which he defined as a process in which "leaders and followers raise one another to higher levels of morality and motivation" (1978, 20). I think of transformational leaders as those who can do three things.

First, they lead their teams and organizations through extraordinary changes and achievements. Second, these leaders are good at getting their team members to align around a shared and often cocreated vision. Third, not only does the organization transform and overachieve, but the team members are also transformed in the process, reaching heights they never thought they could. We'll talk more about this, but let's first understand what is at the core of these great leaders.

One critical aspect of transformational leadership, and for great entrepreneurial leaders, is mindset. Your mindset refers to the collection of beliefs, attitudes, and assumptions you hold about yourself and the world around you (Dweck 2006). It's the mental lens through which you interpret experiences, respond to challenges, and pursue goals. One of the most influential thinkers on this topic is Carol Dweck. She wrote about a fixed mindset versus a growth mindset, and here's how that is important.

A leader with a fixed mindset is likely to believe that abilities and intelligence are static traits. That leader is likely to avoid challenges and fear failure. A leader with a growth mindset, on the other hand, is likely to believe that abilities can be developed through effort, feedback, and persistence (Kouzes and Posner 2019). This leader seeks challenges and sees failure as part of learning. You see where I'm going with this.

Which mindset is an entrepreneurial leader likely to have? It's a growth mindset, for sure. When asked if they've achieved a key goal, they are much more likely to answer with a phrase like *not yet* rather than *no*, suggesting that, in their mind, they are continually on a path of progress.

Several other helpful mindsets are worth considering in this context. For example, a leader with an abundance mindset is likely to believe that there are plenty of opportunities for everyone (Young Entrepreneur Council 2018). This type of leader tends to be more collaborative and optimistic.

A leader with an ownership mindset is likely to take full responsibility for results (Leighton 2021). They don't blame others and are more proactive. A leader with a resilient/anti-fragile mindset is likely to thrive on adversity and is someone who learns and grows stronger through stress (Lee 2025). Even more to the point of entrepreneurial leadership, George Couros (2015) wrote about the innovator's mindset, which characterizes a leader who encourages creativity, risk-taking, and looking at problems as opportunities to improve.

An example of a good mindset is Linda Alvarado, president and CEO of Alvarado Construction. She is the first Latinx owner of a Major League Baseball (MLB) team, the Colorado Rockies. She is a self-made entrepreneur in a male-dominated industry (construction). Alvarado is a longtime advocate for women and minority-owned businesses. Her story aligns with our emphasis here on an entrepreneurial mindset, risk tolerance, and vision, especially in uncharted or exclusionary environments. As a Latinx MLB owner, she embodies the idea of *creating more*—not just through business ventures, but by reshaping what's possible for others.

You can see that the mindset plays an important role in the makeup of an entrepreneurial leader. I can't imagine a successful entrepreneurial leader who doesn't have a growth mindset or an abundance mindset, who is resilient, and who is OK with taking a calculated risk. But I think that we must look a little deeper under the hood for the mindset concept to really understand the value it has to understand the entrepreneurial leader who is, or can be, transformational—the leader who can move mountains, whether launching a start-up that becomes a $1 billion unicorn or leading large-scale, fundamental change within an existing organization. So, let's take a deeper look at the mindset and, in particular, two important elements: ethos and persona.

The Entrepreneurial Ethos and Persona

Ethos refers to a person's character, credibility, and values—in this case, that person is a leader. It's one of Aristotle's three modes of persuasion (alongside pathos and logos), and in leadership, it plays a crucial role in establishing trust and influence. Remember that trust and influence are at the core of what it means to be a leader (Hannah et al. 2011).

In the context of leadership, ethos includes several important ingredients (Hannah and Avolio 2011). The first is credibility, which encompasses the leader's experience, knowledge, and qualifications. Next is integrity, defined as the extent to which the leader acts consistently with their core values and ethical principles. Then comes authenticity: Is the leader genuine and transparent, not putting on a false front? Also important is reputation, which can be seen as what others think and say about the leader based on their actions over time. Finally, there is moral authority, reflecting the leader's commitment to doing what's right, even when it's hard. In a nutshell, ethos is the stuff inside the leader—what makes them tick and drives them to excel and achieve.

A leader with a strong ethos doesn't just *tell* people what to do—they *inspire* trust because of who they are and how they lead. Their character carries weight. Think of someone like Nelson Mandela or Abraham Lincoln. People followed them not just for their ideas but because of the *kind of people they were.*

CREATE MORE LESSON:

A leader with a strong ethos doesn't just tell people what to do—they inspire trust because of who they are and how they lead.

While ethos is about what's inside the leader and how that drives them, persona is more about how people perceive the leader. A leader's persona is the outward expression of their leadership identity—the way they present themselves, communicate, and interact with others (Marshall and Barbour 2015). It's how they are perceived by their team, stakeholders, and the public. While ethos refers to their deeper character and credibility, persona is more about their leadership style, demeanor, and presence (Sohmen 2015).

Among the key elements of a leader's persona is their communication style. How does the leader speak, listen, and engage (e.g., direct and decisive versus empathetic and collaborative)? Next is their presence and demeanor. That includes their confidence, body language, and the way they carry themselves in meetings or public appearances.

We might also consider the leader's emotional tone. Are they calm under pressure, passionate, inspiring, or reserved? Their persona may also be expressed in their decision-making approach. Do they project certainty, seek consensus, or show flexibility? Another important characteristic is the leader's symbolism and image, which includes how they dress, the environments they create, and the narratives they cultivate about themselves. Finally, we might consider the leader's consistency and authenticity. Do they present a genuine version of themselves, or is there a gap between their public persona and private actions?

Let's examine some sample leader personas to drive the point home. Earlier, we discussed the persona of Steve Jobs, who was a bold, charismatic, and future-focused visionary. Abraham Lincoln's persona as a servant leader was humble, empathetic, and people-first. Elon Musk is perceived as a warrior who is relentless, aggressive, and driven. Dwight Eisenhower was regarded as a diplomatic, composed, and wise statesman.

How about another modern business example with Mellody Hobson, co-CEO of Ariel Investments, former chair of the board at Starbucks, former chairperson of DreamWorks, and part owner of the Denver Broncos. She is known for leading with clarity, calm, and a strong sense of values—an example of ethos in action. She often emphasizes the importance of trusted advisors and listening deeply before making decisions. She advocates for shared leadership and power, as seen in her long-standing co-leadership of Ariel with John Rogers, Jr. She helps organizations navigate tough moments through transparency, empathy, and accountability. She is seen as a strong voice for racial equity and inclusive leadership in corporate spaces. Finally, she believes good leadership is about asking the right questions and staying grounded in purpose—not about having all the answers.

The more successful leaders like Hobson have alignment between their persona and their ethos, ensuring that they live true to their values and that they are driven by those values in how they act and lead. They are careful to project an image that reflects their true values and leadership philosophy. Team members and customers can see the alignment, and it matters. This is the aligned mindset of an effective leader and is essential to any leader becoming transformational.

CREATE MORE LESSON:

Successful leaders have alignment between their persona and ethos, ensuring they live true to their values.

As I mentioned above, a transformational leader is someone who inspires and motivates others to achieve more than they thought possible—not just by setting goals but by transforming the beliefs, values, and behaviors of the people they lead. These individuals lead through vision, inspiration, integrity, and personal connection, helping individuals and organizations grow, innovate, and adapt (Bass and Riggio 2006). Their mindset, the roots of which we described as ethos and persona, is all aimed at helping and inspiring their teams and organizations to overachieve.

These leaders are visionary, inspirational, authentic, and supportive. They effectively challenge their team members to think and act differently, innovate, and go beyond the status quo (Deng et al. 2023).

I'm reminded of the work on transformational leadership by James MacGregor Burns (2003) and Bernard Bass (Bass and Riggio 2006). They talked about the four I's of transformational leadership. First, idealized influence is the notion that the leader acts as a role model and builds trust and admiration. Second, inspirational motivation is the idea that the leader creates enthusiasm and commitment around a vision. Third, intellectual stimulation is the concept that the leader promotes creativity and problem-solving. Fourth, individualized consideration is the notion that the leader cares about each team member's development.

This all matters because transformational leaders can drive real change in organizations, not just short-term results. These leaders foster engaged teams and strong cultures. They encourage innovation, especially during times of uncertainty or disruption (Deng et al. 2023). They also leave behind a legacy of leadership by developing other leaders. A transformational leader is not just someone people work for—they are someone people grow because of.

CREATE MORE LESSON:

A transformational leader is not just someone people work for—they are someone people grow because of.

One other key component worth mentioning here is the characteristic of empathy. Empathy is *core* to transformational leadership, especially for entrepreneurial or intrapreneurial leaders who are trying to rally others around a bold vision (Miller 2009). Let's think about the role that empathy plays in transformational leadership.

First, empathy builds trust, which is the foundation for transformation. Transformational leaders often ask teams to follow them into uncertainty. Empathy is the ability to understand and genuinely care about others' perspectives, and it helps build the psychological safety and trust needed for people to take those leaps (Meyer et al. 2016). Whether you're launching a start-up or innovating from within, people won't risk much unless they feel seen, heard, and supported.

Second, empathy fuels inspiration, not just direction. Traditional leadership might focus on giving orders; transformational leadership inspires. That inspiration often stems from knowing what motivates each team member, such as their values, struggles, and aspirations. Empathy allows leaders to *speak to the heart*, not just the job description (Meinecke and Kauffeld 2018).

Third, empathy enhances vision-setting and adaptability. A transformational leader's vision isn't created in a vacuum. Empathetic leaders *cocreate* visions with their teams because they are attuned to others' lived realities. They also adapt their strategies as feedback and need shift, not out of weakness but out of responsiveness (Kalshoven et al. 2013).

Fourth, empathy drives individualized consideration. This is one of the four components of transformational leadership (per Bass and Avolio 1993, 1994): treating each team member as a unique individual. Empathetic leaders understand that not everyone requires the same kind of support or challenge to grow, and they act accordingly.

Fifth, empathy helps navigate resistance and change. Change can be uncomfortable in start-ups and large organizations. Empathy allows leaders to understand why someone might be resisting—fear of obsolescence, uncertainty, or misalignment—and to guide them through it rather than push them aside (Li et al. 2019).

Here's a very important final point on empathy in leadership. *Empathy isn't just emotional intelligence; it's strategic intelligence.* It allows entrepreneurial and intrapreneurial leaders to unleash potential, navigate complexity, and turn vision into action by meeting people where they are (Muss et al. 2025).

CREATE MORE LESSON:

Empathy isn't just emotional intelligence; it's strategic intelligence.

As you can see, we're leaning heavily on my OB training here. Let's pull in one more related concept that will wrap this up nicely. That's the notion of charismatic leadership and how it connects to transformational leadership, especially in the context of entrepreneurs and intrapreneurs. I believe that charismatic leadership is the spark within transformational leadership.

Charisma often gets mistaken for style, such as the magnetism of a confident speaker or the boldness of a founder with swagger. But in the context of transformational leadership, charisma isn't just *presence*; it's *purpose-driven presence* (Avolio and Yammarino 2013). Let's tease that apart to make sure we understand it right.

First, charisma is a catalyst for vision. Charismatic leaders ignite belief. They communicate a compelling vision with conviction and clarity, making others feel like they're part of something extraordinary. This is especially powerful for start-ups or innovation teams inside large companies, as people need to *feel* the vision before they buy in (Hinkin and Tracey 1999).

Second, it's not just charm. It's credibility. Charismatic leadership works best when it's grounded in authenticity and competence (Williams et al. 2018). When leaders walk their talk, show vulnerability, and truly believe in their mission, their charisma becomes contagious. Empty showmanship, on the other hand, fades fast, especially with today's teams, which value transparency.

Third, charisma helps sustain momentum. When you're building something new, whether it's a scrappy start-up or a disruptive internal initiative, there are inevitable dips: setbacks, doubts, and resistance. Charisma helps leaders rally the team, rekindle excitement, and keep moving forward even when the outcome is unclear.

Fourth, charisma without empathy can derail. This is where it ties back to *transformational* leadership. Charisma alone can attract people, but empathy, integrity, and vision keep them engaged for the long haul. True transformation requires more than energy. It needs emotional connection and moral direction.

The quick takeaway here is that *charisma is the accelerant, not the engine*. In transformational leadership, charisma helps generate belief, but empathy, vision, and integrity turn that belief into real and lasting change. Let's look at someone who embodies both charisma and empathy in a deeply grounded way. Our case in point will be Sara Blakely, who blends quiet charisma very well with deep empathy.

CREATE MORE LESSON:

Charisma is the accelerant, not the engine.

Sara Blakely, founder of Spanx, may not fit the traditional image of a charismatic leader, but her *quiet charisma* has built a billion-dollar brand and a fiercely loyal team. Here's my take on Blakely in this context:

- **Empathy-driven innovation:** She created Spanx by deeply understanding a problem women faced and designing a better solution, not just technically but emotionally. Her product came from empathizing with the customer, and that carried into how she built her company culture.

- **Charisma in authenticity:** Blakely's charisma comes through her authenticity, which includes self-deprecating humor, vulnerability, and transparency. Whether on stage or Instagram, she connects as a *real person*, not just a CEO. That kind of charisma builds long-term trust.
- **Transformational leadership:** Blakely didn't just build a product; she transformed how women feel in their own skin. Internally, she championed a supportive, creative culture in which people could grow—a hallmark of individualized consideration.
- **Paying it forward:** When Blakely sold a majority stake in SPANX, she gave every employee $10,000 and two first-class plane tickets to anywhere in the world, not because she had to, but because she *wanted to acknowledge their role in the journey*. That's empathy in action.

Like many successful transformational leaders, Blakely shows us that charisma doesn't have to be loud. It just has to be real. When paired with empathy, it can transform teams and markets alike.

One other example to drive this point home is Lisa Su, CEO of AMD and a Taiwanese American engineer and tech executive. Su is credited with leading AMD through one of the most significant tech turnarounds in recent history. She identified long-term trends in chip architecture and computing demand—clear *pattern recognition* and *foresight*. Su doubled down on high-performance computing at a time when the company was struggling, showing *courageous decision-making* and the ability to *see around corners*. More to the point, she also models *humble yet high-impact leadership*, aligned with this book's treatment of visionary and quiet charismatic leadership (à la Sara Blakely).

CREATE MORE LESSON:

Charisma doesn't have to be loud; it just has to be real.

I'm no Sarah Blakely, but I've tried hard in certain circumstances in my life to think big and inspire my colleagues to take on ambitious projects. Some examples are getting the entrepreneurship program at WSU ranked in the top twenty-five nationally, helping to rethink tech transfer and commercialization at the University of Arizona and creating Tech Launch Arizona, building several classroom-of-the-future projects across several universities, establishing many online programs, assisting in putting a stadium deal together, launching a medical school, getting UNLV to Carnegie R1 status, and even building the Yuhaaviatam Center for Health Studies at CGU to try to promote more interdisciplinary thinking around public health.

All were ambitious projects for which we had to rally the troops to work together. I suppose that I was trying hard to be a transformational leader or perhaps even, in part, a successful entrepreneurial leader. Time will tell whether that was the case, but it was sure fun trying.

The good news here is that most of these psychological traits we've been discussing don't have to be totally innate and/or born in you; they can be learned and developed (Roberts et al. 2005). Let's end this section by thinking about some things you can do to develop the mindset of a successful transformational leader. The key here is the mindset that we talked about.

Putting Yourself in the Mindset of an Entrepreneurial Leader

Remember the key mindsets we talked about—focused on growth, abundance, and innovation. We also talked about your ethos and persona—the inner values that drive you and how they match the way that you act and, thus, how people perceive you. We talked about empathy as a key component as well. Finally, we talked about charisma as a key final component, but not necessarily charisma as in being a people person, but rather in being credible, authentic, and caring. So, how can you cultivate those things in yourself?

There are several things you can do to develop yourself as a transformational leader. For example, to what extent are you self-aware? Do you notice your inner dialogue? Is it fixed or growth oriented? How do you think about your successes and failures? When you do fail, can you reframe your failure and shift your thinking from *I failed* to *I learned*? Are you surrounding yourself wisely?

Mindsets are contagious, and so you can make sure to be around growth-minded people. Do you frequently and clearly practice gratitude? This can not only foster an abundance mindset and build resilience but can also attract others to want to work with you. Are you setting stretch goals for yourself and your team? Aim high and then aim for progress over perfection. One other suggestion is to do mindset workouts daily. These can include daily journaling, affirmations, visualization, and mindfulness practice. All can help.

One's mindset matters in becoming a transformational leader (Lin et al. 2022). It influences how you lead others, how you handle stress, whether you persist through hard times, how creative and open you are to new ideas, and how much your overall happiness and sense of purpose depend on it. To quote Henry Ford, "Whether you think you can, or you think you can't—you're right."

CREATE MORE LESSON:

Whether you think you can, or you think you can't—you're right. —Henry Ford

Perhaps even more importantly, others will want to follow and work with you. We're all attracted to that leader who aims to move mountains and who is passionate and caring and makes us a key part of the journey. If your primary objective is impactful innovation and change, and you are good at helping others to achieve that and go beyond what they dreamed they could ever accomplish, you'll be well on your way to being a truly transformational leader.

In our next act, let's look at one other key characteristic of successful entrepreneurial leaders. They are not only passionate, inspiring, and caring leaders, but they are also creative and have the ability to see around corners. How is it that some leaders can seem to solve problems so well and, in some cases, predict the future?

ACT FOUR

THE LEADER AS A CREATIVE VISIONARY

IN ACT FOUR, let's consider one final important aspect of a successful entrepreneurial leader: their capability to creatively solve problems and seemingly see around corners. Whether for an entrepreneur or an intrapreneur, this is what separates an entrepreneurial leader from just a good operator or manager.

Creativity: I think that one key component here is that for these leaders, creativity is a core competency (Gupta et al. 2004). Even more to the point, entrepreneurial leaders aren't just solving problems—they're reframing them. They're challenging assumptions, asking *what-if?* constantly, and using constraints as launchpads for innovation. These entrepreneurial leaders don't wait for the path to clear—they create new paths entirely. These leaders can blend *imagination* with *execution*, turning raw ideas into workable solutions and workable solutions into scalable ventures.

CREATE MORE LESSON:

Entrepreneurial leaders aren't just solving problems—they're reframing them.

Pattern recognition: The next characteristic that I see in these leaders involves pattern recognition and intuition. Seeing around corners is often the result of *pattern recognition*, and the leader's accumulated experience, curiosity, and cross-domain exposure allow them to anticipate change before it hits (Baron 2006). They notice weak signals others miss, such as shifts in customer behavior, emerging technologies, and silent frustrations. They ask, *If this trend continues, what happens next?* and then build toward that future before it's obvious to everyone else. Here's a good metaphor to help drive this point home. Where others see a foggy horizon, entrepreneurial leaders see the shape of what's coming, even if it's just a silhouette.

Adaptability: Next, I observe that these leaders thrive in ambiguity (Uhl-Bien and Arena 2018). In both start-ups and internal ventures, entrepreneurial leaders operate in areas where maps don't exist. They remain undaunted by chaos and are able to experiment rapidly, iterate constantly, and use feedback loops as a GPS. They're not deterred by the unknown; they're energized by it.

Discernment: I also see in these leaders that they synthesize, not just analyze. Instead of breaking things down into smaller parts (traditional problem-solving), entrepreneurial leaders *combine* unexpected elements: ideas, technologies, disciplines, and markets (Miller 2020). Think, for example, of the premise underlying Airbnb, which combines trust, tech, and spare bedrooms. As another example, think of an intrapreneur at 3M turning adhesive "failures" into Post-it notes.

Foresight: The final characteristic I see in these leaders is the role of vision in creative leadership. That ability to see around corners is tied to vision. They don't just spot problems; they envision *better realities*. That vision inspires teams to keep solving, keep iterating, and keep pushing boundaries. Entrepreneurial leaders are equal parts inventors, detectives, and explorers. They solve today's problems with tomorrow's thinking and build what others don't yet see (Hoang et al. 2025).

Let's look at examples of an entrepreneur and an intrapreneur who epitomize this ability. First, let's look at Reed Hastings and the Netflix pivot. In the early 2000s, Hastings, cofounder of Netflix, was running a successful DVD-by-mail business. But instead of doubling down on what was working, he saw something most others didn't: *the end of physical media*. Broadband speeds were increasing, piracy was reshaping consumer behavior, and the idea of streaming content, which was still clunky and niche at the time, was gaining quiet momentum.

While Blockbuster and others clung to late fees and retail stores, Hastings pushed Netflix into streaming *before* it was popular and *before* the infrastructure fully supported it. It wasn't just a business pivot; it was a creative redefinition of the entertainment industry. He didn't just solve the problem of renting DVDs; he solved the *future* problem of how people would watch media. Corner seen: the shift from physical to digital content delivery. Creative problem solved: delivering instant access to content before the world was asking for it.

Next, let's look at an example of an intrapreneur with this characteristic, Lisa Lindström at Doberman (later EY Doberman). At Doberman, a Swedish design and innovation firm (now part of EY), Lindström was a managing partner who acted more like an intrapreneur than a traditional executive. She pushed her team to stop thinking like a service agency and start building its own internal products—a bold move in the agency world.

Lindström anticipated a future in which clients wouldn't just want design; they'd want *outcomes*. So, her team built its own digital ventures internally, tested them in-market, and then spun them out or leveraged them to drive new types of client engagements. This transformed the firm from a reactive service provider to a proactive innovation lab. Corner seen: the commoditization of design services and the growing demand for outcome-based partnerships. Creative problem solved: turning an agency into a venture studio and creating value before the client even asks.

Can We Learn How to Do This?

Again, I don't think these are innate traits that one is born with. I firmly believe that these can be learned and honed over time. So, *how can you become the kind of entrepreneurial leader who solves creatively and sees around corners?* Here are some practical ideas for becoming a creative, corner-seeing leader. Think of it as a playbook on creativity for mere mortals.

Not everyone is born with Steve Jobs's intuition or Reed Hastings's foresight. But the good news is that these are learnable mindsets and habits. Here's how aspiring entrepreneurial leaders—whether founders or intrapreneurs—can build that muscle.

The first thing you can do is to train yourself to ask better questions. Great problem-solvers don't start with answers; they start with *curiosity*. They ask questions like *What's really going on here?* or *What's the problem behind the problem?* or *If we removed all assumptions, how else could this work?* A good way to practice this is in meetings, in which you can politely try to play the role of a naive outsider. Ask the question no one wants to ask.

The second thing you can try is to actively go outside your bubble. Innovative thinking often comes from cross-pollination. Read outside your field. Talk to people in unrelated industries. Travel. Try new things. A good way to practice is to go to a lecture, a meetup, or a conference completely unrelated to your current work once a month. Watch how your brain lights up in new ways.

The third thing you can do is to try to make peace with uncertainty. Entrepreneurial leaders are comfortable with not having the full map. They don't need perfect data to act—they need just enough to make an educated leap. A good way to practice is to start small. Take one imperfect idea per week and test it. See what you learn. The goal isn't perfection—it's *progress*.

The fourth recommendation is to develop your pattern recognition abilities. Seeing around corners is often about noticing early signals and connecting the dots more quickly than others. A good way to practice this is to spend fifteen minutes each day scanning headlines, newsletters, and social media trends. Ask, *What patterns are emerging here?* Then, write down two or three predictions just for yourself.

The fifth thing you can do is build a creative habit. Creativity isn't a lightning bolt; it's a *discipline*. Treat it like a workout: Make time, show up, and repeat. A helpful practice is to try the ten-ideas-a-day exercise, made famous by James Altucher. Force yourself to list ten new ideas each morning, even if nine are garbage. It's not about the ideas; it's about training your brain to stretch.

Finally, the sixth suggestion is to surround yourself with future-focused people. Your ability to see new solutions and spot what's next is shaped by who you spend time with. Entrepreneurial thinking is contagious, so choose your influences wisely. For practice on this one, you might start or join a mastermind group, a start-up book club, or even a Slack/Discord community of thinkers and builders.

CREATE MORE LESSON:

You don't have to be a genius to see around corners. You just have to start looking sooner, from more angles, and with an open mind.

The important takeaway here is that you don't have to be a genius to see around corners. You just have to start looking sooner, from more angles, and with an open mind. Below is a handy little daily habits checklist for this. Think of it as the corner-seer's checklist, your daily habits for becoming a more creative, entrepreneurial leader. Use it as a compass to keep yourself (or your team) thinking ahead, solving creatively, and staying sharp.

CURIOSITY AND OBSERVATION

- Ask one what-if or why-not question today.
- Spot one hidden assumption in a problem you're working on.
- Watch for weak signals: Is something small pointing to a big shift?

PATTERN RECOGNITION AND LEARNING

- Scan headlines or trend reports for fifteen minutes.
- Jot down one or two predictions or observations.
- Cross-connect two unrelated ideas, just for fun.

CREATIVITY AND IDEA GENERATION

- List ten new ideas (even wild ones)—for example, businesses, products, or life hacks.
- Reframe a problem: How would a ten-year-old, a nurse, or a hacker solve this?

ACTION AND EXPERIMENTATION

- Make one small move on a rough idea: Test something, talk to someone, or make a sketch.
- Celebrate progress, not perfection.

CONNECTION AND INSPIRATION

- Engage with one person or idea *outside* your bubble.
- Reflect on one moment that sparked your curiosity or insight.

WEEKLY BONUS:

- Attend or watch one thing outside your industry.
- Share a seeing-around-corners insight with your team or write it in your journal.

Creativity, foresight, and innovation aren't lightning bolts; they're habits. Start small, repeat daily, and watch your thinking expand. I've done my share of getting out of jams, solving difficult problems, and having to forecast the future, both in the short and long terms. Some personal examples include achieving a very difficult business school reaccreditation at WSU, figuring out how to continue the great trajectory in rankings for the business school at the University of Arizona while also helping it to become a self-sustaining entity on campus, and reaching Carnegie R1 status for UNLV. The example that sticks with me, however, is one in which I'm not sure that I completely succeeded.

CREATE MORE LESSON:

Creativity, foresight, and innovation aren't lightning bolts; they're habits.

Among my personal experiences, one keeps coming back to me as a good example of what we're talking about in this act. I was so fortunate to be able to cap off my higher education leadership career at the helm of CGU, a member of the very prestigious Claremont Colleges in Southern California. I had never attended or worked at a private school before, but I was blessed to be tapped to be the president of CGU. I often joked that it was like being at an Ivy League school but with much better weather. CGU has a rich history of incredible faculty, students, and programs, such as the Peter F. Drucker and Masatoshi Ito Graduate School of Management.

CGU is a grand, one-hundred-year-old, and still unproven experiment in trying to have a university be comprehensive (offering many subjects and majors) and focused completely and exclusively on graduate education. To make that business model even more difficult, CGU prides itself on small, intimate seminars with great faculty and student exchanges on dynamic and interactive learning, supported by a superb staff in a beautiful location in Claremont. This means all grad students, all the time, with no undergrads and no distractions, including sports. We simply focus on the success of grad students in pursuit of world-class master's degrees, doctorates, and certificates, as well as custom, noncredit executive programs that we build and deliver on demand for clients as needed.

CGU is also transdisciplinary at its core, which means that students are able to study without limits, boundaries, or borders. I would say that CGU is relatively applied, which means that faculty members are working on real-world problems with real people out in the world, with students working alongside faculty on very practical problems. CGU also draws from an incredibly smart, driven, and diverse set of students from all over the world, who want small courses and personal attention, plus a focus on student success.

Many people and services are aimed at making sure students succeed. Finally, CGU is built on a liberal arts tradition that has attracted many great faculty members over the decades, such as the business guru Peter Drucker, as well as Mihaly Csikszentmihalyi, the Hungarian American psychologist who coined the concept of flow, that optimal state of deep focus and immersion.

CGU is also a member of the Claremont Colleges, which is a group of seven great colleges in a somewhat unique consortium built on the Cambridge and Oxford models. These are separate colleges that are colocated and share some important services, such as campus safety, a beautiful library, and an underlying financial management system. Tucked together in the foothills of the San Gabriel Mountains about thirty or so miles inland from downtown Los Angeles—what could be better than that?

When I stepped into leadership at CGU, higher education was already facing serious headwinds. These pressures haven't eased. In fact, they represent some of the most disruptive forces I've seen in my thirty-five-year career.

Globalization has significantly altered the playing field. Countries around the world have been heavily investing in their own colleges and universities, so international students no longer feel compelled to come to the US for a quality education. On top of that, visa delays and bureaucratic hurdles are still making it difficult for many students to get into US institutions (Altbach and De Wit 2018).

Technological change has also been a relentless force. For more than twenty years, the rise of automation and digital tools has reshaped how people engage with education. This shift toward online learning and hybrid models has created a strong expectation for convenience and flexibility (Times Higher Education 2023). Students now expect education to fit into their lives, not the other way around.

Demographics are another major challenge. We're now dealing with the consequences of a national decline in birth rates, and the demographic cliff is no longer a theory—it's here. There are simply fewer eighteen-year-olds entering college. While population growth in countries such as India does present opportunities, many of those students now have solid educational options at home and elsewhere. The US is no longer the only game in town (Tasneem 2019).

At the same time, the value of a traditional college degree is being questioned more than ever. Young adults are increasingly exploring alternative paths, from online certificates outside traditional higher education to launching careers directly through start-ups or influencer platforms. As a result, universities are being pushed to unbundle their offerings and present education in more digestible, targeted ways (Gallup and Lumina Foundation 2024).

Price is another sticking point. The cost of earning a college degree continues to climb, and on some campuses, it's simply exorbitant. Most schools are under intense pressure to cut spending, and price sensitivity is becoming a major factor in program decisions. Institutions are being forced to rethink their budgets and pricing models just to stay competitive (Kelchen 2023).

There's also been a shift in how universities staff their faculties. More and more institutions are hiring fewer tenure-track professors with PhDs and are instead leaning on adjuncts, part-time instructors, and clinical faculty. At the same time, class sizes have increased. This trend—what some call adjunctification—is changing the academic labor landscape and impacting the student experience (Kezar et al. 2019).

Privatization has entered the conversation as well. Whether public or private, universities are beginning to operate more like businesses. State schools are admitting more out-of-state and international students because they pay higher tuition. College athletics at the Division 1 level are negotiating huge name, image, and likeness deals. Institutions are pushing hard to boost revenue from auxiliary operations, such as student housing, and to tap into tech transfer and commercialization opportunities (American Association of State Colleges and Universities 2023).

And of course, politics has become a more powerful force on campus than ever before. My final semester at CGU happened to coincide with a period in which university presidents from highly respected institutions were being called to testify before Congress. Some of them even lost their positions as a result (American Association of University Professors 2024).

All of this disruption was anticipated by Clayton Christensen of Harvard Business School, who wrote extensively about how higher education would be upended by market shifts (Christensen and Eyring 2011). What's happening now is essentially a transition from a seller's market to a buyer's market. The power is shifting from institutions to students, who now have more choices, more leverage, and greater expectations.

The questions we keep returning to are *How durable are these forces?* and *Are any of them going away soon?* When you really look at it, none of them appear to be reversing. If anything, they are intensifying. Ratings agencies have even noted that with nearly six thousand institutions in the federal higher education database, the market is oversaturated. In a contracting market, consolidation seems not only likely but inevitable.

Thinking Outside the Box at CGU

So, at CGU, we had to think outside the box and look around corners to peek into the future of higher education as we made vital decisions about the future of the university. That prompted a fundamental rethinking of our business model. We asked the basic questions that Drucker (2008) was famous for, including who we were, who our customers were, what our product was, and why our customers liked our product vis-à-vis those of our competitors. We had to rethink everything, given what was going on in the industry and the disruption that Christensen talked about.

We had to come up with new ways to generate revenue, new programs, new modalities, even better pathways for student success, new ways of using our facilities, and so on. Everything was on the table. We did not want to be an industry incumbent—one of the old, stalwart institutions that Christensen predicted often go the way of the buggy whip. We knew we needed to innovate or go out of business.

The good news is that we took a hard look at ourselves and conducted extensive research on the developments occurring both regionally and nationally within our industry. While we recognized our relative smallness, we also discovered that we were surprisingly agile and entrepreneurial, allowing us to pivot and guide others into a bold new era of transformative graduate education. We ventured online for the first time at the university even before the pandemic lockdown required it.

In fact, we turned to Arizona State University for help in designing an online master's program in public health, and to this day, it does very well. We reimagined the doctorate, offering many new professional doctorates that were much more applied, took less time to complete, and could be attended in a hybrid format. We devised new approaches to marketing, recruiting, and admissions, literally rethinking everything from the bottom up in terms of our relationship with our students from beginning to end. We cut costs and held off on raising tuition for several years. We also brought in more than $100 million in new outside funding to help fuel our vision for the future.

Our strongest headwind was perhaps of our own making. We were small, nimble, and entrepreneurial, but we were also steeped in a storied history and a thick organizational culture that sometimes got in our way. We found it helpful to go back to our early roots, when our founder, James Blaisdell, felt that the new, fledgling graduate offerings might get in the way of the Pomona College undergraduate students' success.

As a result, he not only spun out an all-graduate start-up university (CGU), but in the process, he also helped to create a groundbreaking college consortium based on models at Oxford and Cambridge. That was some heady, innovative stuff, wouldn't you say? We were born out of radical innovation and a strong entrepreneurial mindset more than one hundred years ago, and this is still there, deep within CGU's DNA.

Accordingly, we had to find a way to dig back into our DNA and our past and back beyond small, intimate seminars with great faculty members, transdisciplinarity, applied teaching and research, our great location, and everything else that we'd been known for in our immediate past. While holding on to those more recent strengths, we had to find a way to get back to flexing that old muscle that Blaisdell had and exercised so well at the start. We needed to find entrepreneurial leadership again, some one hundred years later.

The hundred-year-old CGU experiment in transformative graduate education continues to this day. I'd like to think that I left it better than I found it. We certainly grew enrollment in many of these new programs. Like much of higher education right now, the CGU experiment continues and is yet unproven.

For those who seek to be great entrepreneurial leaders, they must find a way to solve problems creatively and to get at least a glimpse or sense of what the future might be like. I hope this section helped you find a pathway toward developing your own creativity and vision. In the final act, let's think about why this is all so vitally important. Why do we need entrepreneurial leaders now more than ever?

ACT FIVE

THE LEADER WE NEED

I BELIEVE THAT THE WORLD needs entrepreneurial leaders now more than ever. We need them to continue starting great new companies and fixing broken mature ones. I think that extends to all types of organizations, including those in government, schools, universities, and everywhere else where we see broken, bloated, and wasteful organizations.

What I find interesting is that the US was built to create and inspire this kind of leadership. Yes, that's right. The US was built for this. We very mindfully set up a system of helpful rules for entrepreneurs, created innovation engines, and put in place some important incentives for entrepreneurship in this country. Think about it more carefully, and you'll see what I mean.

We created powerful intellectual property protection in the form of patents and related laws that help you protect your ideas. That doesn't happen everywhere in the world, and it was perfected early in our country. We also created helpful bankruptcy laws that made it OK to fail in a business venture. That permission to fail made it easier for entrepreneurs to take risks and created a culture in this country in which business failure is accepted and even heralded in some entrepreneurial sectors. We created a system of tax laws that allows entrepreneurs to benefit financially from their hard work and creativity and pay income, company, and capital gains taxes that are significantly less than they are in other developed countries. All these entrepreneurial advantages were built into the model practically from inception here in the US.

We later made huge investments in the engines of innovation, namely our K–12 system and our higher education institutions. All served to produce bright, eager entrepreneurs to take advantage of the rules and incentives we had put in place for everyone. Our investment in research-intensive universities—in particular, our state-supported AAU and Carnegie R1 universities—created innovation ecosystems and literal idea factories across the country that are, to this day, the envy of the world. These investments helped to create some of the best innovation hubs in the world in places such as Silicon Valley, Austin, and Boston, and later in areas such as La Jolla, California; Salt Lake City, Utah; and even my own Las Vegas, Nevada (ranked by Dealroom as being in the top five of US-based cities by annual growth in investment in start-ups).

Similarly, we invested heavily in government programs at all levels to help promote and enable entrepreneurs. For example, at the federal level, we have the Small Business Innovation Research and Small Business Technology Transfer grants, which offer nondilutive funding for R&D-intensive start-ups, with funding coming federally from the likes of the National Institutes of Health, Department of Defense, National Science Foundation, Department of Energy, and others. We have the US Small Business Administration, which provides loans and grants to small businesses and gives advice through the Service Corps of Retired Executives and Small Business Development Centers networks. The US Economic Development Administration has its Build to Scale program, which provides grants for innovation hubs, accelerators, and venture development. The list goes on, and suffice it to say that we offer far more to entrepreneurs at the federal level than any country in the world.

Along these same lines, states provide various forms of additional support to entrepreneurs. In my state of Nevada, for example, our Nevada Governor's Office of Economic Development offers innovation-based incentives, tax abatements, and State Small Business Credit Initiative deployment. We also have the Battle Born Growth fund, a state-sponsored venture capital initiative. Here in Clark County and within the cities of Las Vegas and Henderson, we also provide numerous services and extensive support programs for entrepreneurs. Additionally, local universities, such as UNLV, offer valuable programming, including UNLV's Black Fire Innovation, a hub dedicated to supporting tech commercialization and start-ups.

You can find similar offerings in states across the country. My point is that we built this country from the ground up as an entrepreneur's paradise in large part because of our US founders reacting to Great Britain's business and personal restrictions that they rebelled against. While we've had fits and starts as a country, it's hard to argue that the entrepreneurial stuff we baked into the cake didn't work. The US economy is still the largest globally, with a GDP of around $26.7 trillion in 2024, maintaining its position (International Monetary Fund 2024). China follows as the second largest, with a GDP of approximately $17.7 trillion, but the US remains ahead by a significant margin.

What's even more important, the US still holds the dominant position as the best innovation economy, for all the reasons I described above. Our tech hubs still lead the way. We're still home to many, if not most, of the world's largest tech companies, such as Apple, Google, Microsoft, and Tesla, among others. The US has the most developed venture capital ecosystem, which is crucial for funding high-risk innovation, especially in tech and biotech.

The US also continues to be the home of most of the world's top research universities, including the Massachusetts Institute of Technology, Stanford University, Harvard University, and the University of California, Berkeley, which continue to foster research, start-up incubation, and talent development in innovation. Similarly, our United States Patent and Trademark Office also leads globally in patent filings and intellectual property protections, essential for protecting and scaling new technologies (World Intellectual Property Organization 2024). This is clearly a country built for entrepreneurs, and despite our obvious deficiencies, it has created the world's best innovation-based economy.

Are We Losing Our Entrepreneurial Edge?

While the US remains a leader in innovation, some challenges have emerged. China is rapidly closing the gap, particularly in areas such as AI, 5G technology, and green energy. China's state-backed innovation initiatives (e.g., Made in China 2025) have led to huge investments in R&D and technological advancements. We also continue to see rising competitors in Europe and Asia.

Germany and France, for example, have made strides in clean energy innovation. South Korea and Japan continue to lead in robotics, electronics, and manufacturing automation. India is gaining attention for its booming tech ecosystem, especially in fintech and AI.

In fact, some critics argue that the US could innovate more efficiently if it streamlined regulations, particularly around things such as healthcare innovation or energy transition policies. Overregulation in certain sectors could potentially slow down the pace of some innovative fields.

The important conclusion here is that, to borrow a prior tagline from Ford Motor Company, the best never rest. The US is still the largest economy and remains one of the best innovation economies because of its entrepreneurial ecosystem, funding mechanisms, research capacity, and talent pool. However, rising competition from countries such as China and various European and Asian nations indicates that the global landscape is becoming more competitive.

Innovation in the US is still strong, but staying at the top requires renewed focus on improving policy frameworks and accelerating investments in emerging technologies, including AI, quantum computing, and clean tech. We've got to continue to support and incentivize our young entrepreneurs and intrapreneurs.

CREATE MORE LESSON:

We've got to continue to support and incentivize our young entrepreneurs and intrapreneurs.

The other reason that is also important is that this entrepreneurial ecosystem writ large expands the pie, creating more for everyone—a true win-win economically. I'm reminded of the Captain James T. Kirk quote from *Star Trek*: "to boldly go where no man has gone before!" That quote was later appropriately updated in a subsequent

Star Trek series to say "where *no one* has gone before." There was an even better and more relevant Captain Kirk quote, however, that is more to the point.

Kirk famously said, "I don't believe in the no-win scenario" in the *Star Trek: The Wrath of Khan* (1982) movie. This line occurs during a key moment when Kirk and his crew face an extremely difficult challenge: a seemingly impossible test in Starfleet's Kobayashi Maru simulation.

In the Kobayashi Maru simulation, cadets are presented with a no-win scenario in which the Kobayashi Maru, a civilian ship, is stranded in the Klingon Neutral Zone. Starfleet officers must decide between saving the ship and avoiding war with the Klingons. The simulation is designed to test the cadets' ethics, leadership, and decision-making under pressure. The trick is that there is no way to win, as both options lead to dire consequences.

Kirk, a character known for his leadership, creative problem-solving, and refusal to accept defeat, reprograms the simulation so that he can win. When asked about his actions, he responds with the line, "I don't believe in the no-win scenario." Now, let me recognize, for all the Trekkies out there, that in the 2009 *Star Trek* reboot directed by J. J. Abrams, Chris Pine's Kirk says the same line when he reprograms the Kobayashi Maru test in the modern reimagining of the *Star Trek* universe. This was a homage to the original *Wrath of Khan* moment, but it was presented in the new timeline and context of the rebooted franchise.

In any event, what does it mean? Kirk's belief is rooted in his refusal to accept defeat and his inherent belief that there's always a way out of seemingly impossible situations. In his view, a no-win scenario is not a true test of character or leadership. Instead, it's about finding a creative solution, even when the odds seem insurmountable.

This line is often cited as emblematic of Kirk's character: bold, determined, and resourceful. It's one of the core principles that define his leadership style. He doesn't see failure as an option but instead pushes to innovate and adapt, often in unconventional ways. This line also reflects an optimistic outlook that no challenge is completely without hope and that there is always a way to navigate tough situations. It shows Kirk's refusal to accept predetermined boundaries or limits. For him, leadership is about pushing past what's expected and coming up with new solutions to problems, even in dire circumstances.

In a broader sense, this phrase is often adopted in leadership and motivational contexts to convey the idea of perseverance, adaptability, and the power of creativity in overcoming obstacles. For me, it beautifully illustrates the very entrepreneurial spirit that this country was built on and needs to this day.

CREATE MORE LESSON:

Entrepreneurial leaders don't take no for an answer, and even in impossible situations, they find the possible.

Now, let's make this personal. Honestly, wouldn't you rather work for this kind of leader? More to the point, wouldn't you rather be this kind of leader? I'm guessing that the answer is yes. We are drawn to these types of leaders, and many of us aspire to be this kind of leader.

Sadly, there is a bit of an assault on that leadership archetype right now, as if it is a bad thing to be a successful entrepreneur and generate wealth. Frankly, I find that sad, worrisome, and counterproductive. We need to be very careful about this, as it tears into the very fabric of what makes this country great, not only in terms of value creation but also in terms of philanthropy and giving wealth away for the good of all. I see entrepreneurship as the great equalizer, open and available to all, no matter their background or formal education.

I love to go back and watch online that inspiring and iconic 1997 Apple "Think Different" commercial narrated by Richard Dreyfuss and featuring the line "Here's to the crazy ones." I encourage you to watch it on YouTube. This ad celebrates individuals who challenge the status quo and drive innovation.

The commercial is thought to have been created and inspired by Steve Jobs, and it is thought to have played a key part in saving Apple from going bankrupt. After the release of Microsoft's Windows 95, Apple fell into a death spiral. By September 1997, the company was just two months away from bankruptcy. Fired in 1985, Jobs agreed to return in 1997 as interim CEO. His vision and bold decisions would be crucial in saving Apple, and that ad from 1997 was as much a salute to him as it was to entrepreneurs everywhere (Isaacson 2011). The ad is powerful and sums up the point of this final act in this book very well.

And Now the Bad News

Before I conclude the final act, I must deal with one last delicate topic. So far, I've steadfastly maintained that entrepreneurial leadership can be developed and honed. The truth is that it is a bit more complicated. Let me explain what I mean. I've got one important caveat that I'll now explain, and it deals with our inherent tolerance of risk.

The potential downside of all this is that all that training and preparation won't amount to much if you lack one essential personality trait: your tolerance for risk. Research on successful entrepreneurs shows that they tend to have a somewhat higher tolerance for risk than other people (Hvide and Panos 2014). It's not that they are willing to take reckless risks. Quite the contrary; they excel at closely analyzing risks and then taking careful, calculated risks when they deem them necessary and beneficial.

Most people don't innately possess those decision-making skills, and even if they acquire them, they often reach the end of that decision-making process without the stomach to roll the dice and take that risk by acting on their idea, whether it's by leaving their day job, launching a company based on their concept, betting their savings on their start-up, pivoting the start-up to keep it alive, or seeking investments from others. So, can this risk-taking element be learned, or is it innate? Can it be measured and developed? Well, yes and no. Let me explain.

This brings me back to one of the undergraduate courses I really loved to teach and in which I got my best teaching evaluations consistently. It was a course on, no surprise, entrepreneurial leadership. I taught it to undergrads in the College of Business and Economics (now the Carson College of Business) at WSU. All business undergraduates, no matter what business area they majored in, were required to take this course (or at least had it as one of multiple choices to satisfy a requirement), and so I had a steady supply of business students every year who needed the course, plus students we attracted from adjacent areas. They came from every undergraduate business major you could imagine, including accounting, finance, management and strategy, operations management, MIS, marketing, business analytics, international business, supply chain management, economics, hospitality, real estate, personnel/HR management, and, of course, entrepreneurship.

Each time I taught that course early in the semester, I had the students participate in an exercise that helped them understand not only what it meant to be an entrepreneur but also whether they were likely to become one. And if they weren't, I guided them on how they could work with entrepreneurs to achieve success. To start, I had the students complete a general personality inventory, such as the Myers-Briggs Type Indicator (Randall et al. 2017), and invited a professional to help debrief the results with the class. I also had them fill out a more general inventory on personal strengths and passions, such as the StrengthsFinder index, before debriefing on that as well.

Next, the students completed a leadership inventory, such as the Leadership Practices Inventory by Kouzes and Posner (2003), followed by a comprehensive debrief conversation. Then, I had them fill out an inventory focused on entrepreneurship, such as the Entrepreneurial Mindset Profile developed at the Leadership Development Institute at Eckerd College (Davis et al. 2016). Finally, to emphasize how entrepreneurs think, the students completed an in-depth psychometric inventory called the preference for procedural order (PPO), developed by Linda Putnam (1979). This last inventory was particularly valuable for helping the students understand their inclination toward structured and organized approaches in group settings. That one was incredibly helpful!

The PPO scale was helpful for students in determining whether they had high or low PPO. High-PPO individuals prefer planned and sequential task activities, emphasize time management and predictability, focus on clarifying group procedures, and ensure adherence to tasks. Low-PPO individuals, on the other hand, favor flexibility and adaptability in plans, are less concerned with strict time constraints, and balance task objectives with the group's socio-emotional needs. Well, you can probably see where I am going with this.

Each semester, in that course, I would have the students fill out the PPO and calculate their results, and I would have them move their desks from one side of the classroom to the other based on their PPO scores, from low to high. The result was that each student would be sitting at their desk, from one end of the room to the other, all in order from left to right by their PPO scores. And then, as we debriefed, we would watch their apertures open!

Every time I used that inventory in this class and lined up the students from low PPO to high PPO, I had them call out their majors, from one side of the room to the other. And every time I did that, they discovered they were lined up neatly by their majors, in nearly perfect groupings, and in the same order by major every semester. As you might expect, the accounting majors were all high PPO and were in a cluster at one end of the classroom, and the entrepreneurship majors were nearly all low PPO, neatly assembled together at the other end of the classroom. Majors such as marketing also tended to be low PPO and sat together near the entrepreneur majors, though not quite at that extreme. Similarly, most MIS, operations, statistics, analytics, and corporate finance majors tended to be high PPO and sat in clusters at the side of the room heading toward and/or near the accounting majors, though also not quite at that extreme.

It worked like clockwork every time I did that exercise, and it enabled some incredible conversations between students from different majors. I asked them to explain why they had these preferences, what they thought they were based on, why they were important to them, what it felt like to be in situations that didn't match their preferences, and what it was like to work with others with different preferences. As you might expect, the conversations were enlightening and helped them to better understand each other and how best to work with each other.

I would joke that if the students ended up working together within the same organizations later, the people at the extreme left side of the room (i.e., the entrepreneurs) would be asking for money for projects within their organizations, and the people at the right side of the room (i.e., the accounting and finance majors) would have to approve it. They would nod in agreement and laugh. I would go on to say that the gatekeepers on the right side of the room would likely scoff at the entrepreneurial folks on the left, but they would need them to advance and grow the business. Similarly, the people on the left would probably return the favor and scoff at the folks on the right, but they would need them to breathe life into their entrepreneurial ideas. These were great conversations, and the students learned so much about what it means to be, work with, and support entrepreneurs. Apertures opened.

So, call it what you want: PPO, tolerance for ambiguity, or simply the ability to be flexible. At the end of the day, the successful entrepreneur is also eventually going to need to take a risk and be able to accept that. Now, some of those entrepreneurship majors had backgrounds, upbringings, training, and role models much like I did, but they also tended to have a higher tolerance for risk. To help tease this out, I also used behavioral decision-making exercises in class.

Some of the inventories were applied investment decision-making scenarios, and others were more scientific, often based on the decision-making research of the Nobel Prize–winning economists Tversky and Kahneman (1974). These exercises showed the students that some of them just had a higher tolerance for risk, and others didn't. I could teach them about it and help them develop it, but some just couldn't get there.

These students just weren't wired that way. So, in retrospect, I feel that I could have developed risk tolerance in many of them, but not all. For some, risk-taking was just a bridge too far. For them, it was really a case of nature winning out over nurture. The good news is that my experience as a professor suggests that, for many others whom I've encountered over the decades while teaching entrepreneurship and assisting entrepreneurs, tolerance can be learned and developed. There is hope for budding entrepreneurs.

CREATE MORE LESSON:

Successful entrepreneurs must become comfortable taking risks, and nearly anyone can learn to do this.

All the training and experience I gained from early childhood through graduate school certainly helped me, and I also have a high tolerance for risk. Was I born with it? Perhaps all that preparation helped me develop that tolerance, or maybe it is separate from the experiences I've had and is instead inherent in my DNA. I suppose only my wife, close friends, and family can say for sure. In any event, it certainly worked out for me. As a longtime professor in tech, leadership, and entrepreneurship, and later as a two-time business school dean and two-time university president, those entrepreneurial tendencies were always present. I always saw myself as an innovator, a creative change agent in higher education, and a risk-taker. I also consistently dabbled in entrepreneurial ventures on the side throughout my career (more on that later), and I feel that I am still in that same entrepreneurial frame of mind.

So, you can take some solace in the fact that my experience suggests that risk tolerance can be taught to a certain extent. You can develop ways to take successful calculated risks and become more comfortable with taking risks.

Believe me, this is important for all of us, and it will be personally rewarding for you. We need you to be more entrepreneurial, and it will be worth your while. For the seasoned pros, keep rolling the dice. For the newbies out there, give it a chance and create a great new venture. Also, consider innovating within a mature organization that has lost its way. Think about leaning in and working hard to turn around a mature organization that has run aground. Additionally, consider helping to find ways to improve how we are governed. All of you, keep rolling the dice. We need entrepreneurial leadership now more than ever.

EPILOGUE

I LOVE THAT QUESTION: Wouldn't you rather be this type of leader? Of course you would. We all want to have that opportunity and to find the courage to lead others in something important and impactful. To do something different that makes a huge difference and pulls people together to accomplish it. To help people live to their fullest potential and beyond. To have a positive impact and leave a positive and important legacy.

Toward that end, I've always loved "The Road Not Taken," a famous poem written in 1915 by Robert Frost. I mentioned it briefly earlier in this book. The key ending passage that is relevant to me is, "Two roads diverged in a wood, and I—I took the one less traveled by, And that has made all the difference."

That famous poem and ending line have been interpreted in many ways. Some have argued that Frost was simply teasing a friend of his. But I interpret it my way and take much more serious meaning from the poem and the line. I have chosen to take the road less traveled over and over in my life rather than the safe, well-worn route. And I am so glad that I have. It mattered to me because I felt more happiness and fulfillment in doing so, and I think it also helped me to help others even more than I might have, which, as it turns out, was way more important to me than simply not being bored.

In my prior book on selfless leadership, I discussed the duality in my life and approach to leadership. From my mom, I learned humility and the importance of serving others, aka leading selflessly. From my dad, I learned about entrepreneurship and the necessity of picking myself up by my own bootstraps. These two sides sometimes conflicted, with one part of me knowing the right way to act and wanting to charge ahead, and another part working selflessly and tirelessly to ensure people were heard, engaged, and helped to cocreate our shared vision.

It has been a delicate and challenging leadership balance for me, but I suppose it was exactly what was needed. I am fortunate to have worked with so many talented teams, and we've accomplished so much together. More importantly, the extent to which I have helped others grow and evolve and have inspired them to pursue their own entrepreneurial journeys brings me even greater satisfaction. In the end, I sought to engage, encourage, inspire, and help others find and feel belonging, meaning, and connection, and isn't that what it's all about?

COMING SOON

COMING SOON FROM the award-winning author of *Self Less* and *Create More*, the third installment in the leadership novella series, *End Well: Lessons Learned from a Lifelong Chase for Legacy*. In this third book in the series, Len Jessup dives deep into the popular themes from *Self Less*, including reputation, impact, and legacy. In that upcoming book, Len challenges us all to ask ourselves why we do what we do. What drives our leadership, and what do we want to see when we get to the end of our path and look back at what we've accomplished?

ACKNOWLEDGMENTS

FIRST, LET ME THANK Ezra Byer, Nate Best, and the entire team at Forbes for helping once again in getting my draft manuscript into great shape. Similarly, Jennifer Villalobos was my ace relief pitcher once again, coming into the late innings on this project and helping me find the right references and rethink some of the text.

Fundamentally, however, I must thank my mom and my dad. They are my origin story, and they shaped my approach to life and leadership. My duality of selfless and entrepreneurial leadership stems from both of them, for which I am forever grateful and indebted. This one is dedicated to them, first and foremost.

I also want to give a shout-out to my kids. I enjoyed fun fort-building and other creative play with them when they were little, and they are my most important and inspiring budding entrepreneurs.

And to Kristi, my love, thank you for continuously encouraging me to take on entrepreneurial and intrapreneurial risks, including the significant decision to step away from higher education administration to pursue my entrepreneurial passion.

ABOUT THE AUTHOR

LEN JESSUP IS A TWO-TIME university president, two-time business school dean, longtime business school professor, and a start-up investor and pioneer. Len is also a visionary leader in higher education, known as a consensus builder with a deep interest in innovation, entrepreneurship, leadership, and organizational change. He is managing partner of Desert Forge Ventures, a venture capital firm aimed at promising start-ups in Las Vegas. He was recently president of Claremont Graduate University, a member of the prestigious Claremont College consortium in Southern California. He has also served as president of the University of Nevada, Las Vegas, as well as dean of the business schools at both the University of Arizona and Washington State University, among other senior leadership roles.

In addition to his academic achievements, he has received numerous awards, including the prestigious CEO Award from the Council for Advancement and Support of Education (CASE) District VII. The first in his family to graduate from college, Jessup was born and raised in Northern California. He holds a doctorate in Management and Organizational Behavior from the University of Arizona, with a minor in Management Information Systems. He also holds an MBA as well as a bachelor's degree in information and communication studies, both from California State University, Chico.

REFERENCES

Addy, W. A., A. O. Ajayi-Nifise, B. G. Bello, S. T. Tula, O. Odeyemi, and T. Falaiye. 2024. "Entrepreneurial Leadership in High-Tech Industries: A Review of Key Traits and Success Strategies." *GSC Advanced Research and Reviews* 18, no. 2: 286–96.

Altbach, Philip G., and Hans de Wit. 2018. "The Challenge to Higher Education Internationalisation." *University World News*, February 23, 2018. https://www.universityworldnews.com/post.php?story=20180220091648602. 4.

Amabile, T. M. 1997. "Motivating Creativity in Organizations: On Doing What You Love and Loving What You Do." *California Management Review* 40, no. 1: 39–58. https://doi.org/10.2307/41165921.

American Association of State Colleges and Universities. 2023. *2023 Public Policy Agenda*. https://aascu.org/resources/2023-public-policy-agenda/.

American Association of University Professors. 2024. "Statement on Political Interference in Higher Education." January. https://www.aaup.org/report/statement-political-interference-higher-education.

Antonakis, J., and E. Autio. 2007. "Entrepreneurship and Leadership." In *The Psychology of Entrepreneurship*, edited by J. R. Baum, M. Frese, and R. A. Baron. Routledge.

Antonakis, J., N. Bastardoz, P. Jacquart, and B. Shamir. 2016. "Charisma: An Ill-Defined and Ill-Measured Gift." *Annual Review of Organizational Psychology and Organizational Behavior* 3: 293–319. https://doi.org/10.1146/annurev-orgpsych-041015-062305.

Antoncic, B., and R. D. Hisrich. 2003. "Clarifying the Intrapreneurship Concept." *Journal of Small Business and Enterprise Development* 10, no. 1: 7–24. https://doi.org/10.1108/14626000310461187.

Apple Inc. 1997. *Think Different* [television advertisement; narrated by Richard Dreyfuss]. Directed by Jennifer Golub. In *Think Different (Full Version)*. YouTube video, 1:01. Posted July 11, 2013. https://www.youtube.com/watch?v=5sMBhDv4sik.

Avolio, B. J., and F. J. Yammarino, eds. 2013. "Introduction to, and Overview of, Transformational and Charismatic Leadership." In *Transformational and Charismatic Leadership: The Road Ahead*, 10th anniversary ed. Emerald Group Publishing Limited.

Baird, A., and T. Hedin. 2024. "Entrepreneurship, Startups, and Business Formation Are Booming Across the U.S." *Center for American Progress*, January 19. https://www.americanprogress.org/article/entrepreneurship-startups-and-business-formation-are-booming-across-the-u-s/.

Baron, R. A. 2006. "Opportunity Recognition as Pattern Recognition: How Entrepreneurs 'Connect the Dots' to Identify New Business Opportunities." *Academy of Management Perspectives* 20, no. 1: 104–19.

Bass, B. M., and B. J. Avolio. 1993. "Transformational Leadership and Organizational Culture." *Public Administration Quarterly* 17, no. 1: 112–21. http://www.jstor.org/stable/40862298.

Bass, B. M., and B. J. Avolio. 1994. "Transformational Leadership and Organizational Culture." *International Journal of Public Administration* 17, no. 3–4: 541–54.

Bass, B. M., and R. E. Riggio. 2006. *Transformational Leadership*, 2nd ed. Lawrence Erlbaum Associates.

Blank, Steve. 2012. "The Lean LaunchPad Online." *Steve Blank*, September 6. https://steveblank.com/2012/09/06/the-lean-launchpad-online/.

Blank, Steve. 2013. "Why the Lean Start-Up Changes Everything." *Harvard Business Review* 91, no. 5: 64–72. https://hbr.org/2013/05/why-the-lean-start-up-changes-everything.

Brown, T. 2009. *Change by Design: How Design Thinking Creates New Alternatives for Business and Society*. Harvard Business Press.

Burns, J. M. 1978. *Leadership*. Harper & Row.

Burns, J. M. 2003. *Transforming Leadership: A New Pursuit of Happiness.* Atlantic Monthly Press.

Chernova, Y. 2024. "Pro Take: Here's Why Bargain Hunters Were Stymied This Year in Venture Capital." *Wall Street Journal*, December 24. https://www.wsj.com/articles/pro-take-heres-why-bargain-hunters-were-stymied-this-year-in-venture-capital-a4220b63.

Christensen, C. M., and H. J. Eyring. 2011. *The Innovative University: Changing the DNA of Higher Education from the Inside Out.* Jossey-Bass.

Clearly Payments. 2024. "The Number of Businesses in the USA and Statistics for 2024." January 3. https://www.clearlypayments.com/blog/the-number-of-businesses-in-the-usa-and-statistics-for-2024/.

Couros, G. 2015. *The Innovator's Mindset: Empower Learning, Unleash Talent, and Lead a Culture of Creativity.* Dave Burgess Consulting.

Csikszentmihalyi, M. 1990. *Flow: The Psychology of Optimal Experience.* Harper & Row.

Davis, M. H., J. A. Hall, and P. S. Mayer. 2016. "Developing a New Measure of Entrepreneurial Mindset: Reliability, Validity, and Implications for Practitioners." *Consulting Psychology Journal: Practice and Research* 68, no. 1: 21.

Deng, C., D. Gulseren, C. Isola, K. Grocutt, and N. Turner. 2023. "Transformational Leadership Effectiveness: An Evidence-Based

Primer." *Human Resource Development International* 26, no. 5: 627–41.

Dickel, P., M. Sienknecht, and J. Hörisch. 2021. "The Early Bird Catches the Worm: An Empirical Analysis of Imprinting in Social Entrepreneurship." *Journal of Business Economics* 91, no. 2: 127–50.

Drucker, Peter F. 2008. *The Five Most Important Questions You Will Ever Ask About Your Organization*. Jossey-Bass.

Dweck, C. S. 2006. *Mindset: The New Psychology of Success*. Random House.

Eldor, Karin. "How Saying 'Yes' Can Improve Creativity and Company Culture, According to Doberman Founder Lisa Lindström." *Forbes*, February 11, 2020. https://www.forbes.com/sites/karineldor/2020/02/11/how-saying-yes-can-improve-creativity-and-company-culture-according-to-doberman-founder-lisa-lindstrom/.

Fisher, R., A. Maritz, and A. Lobo. 2016. "Does Individual Resilience Influence Entrepreneurial Success?" *Academy of Entrepreneurship Journal* 22, no. 2: 39–53.

Frost, Robert. "The Road Not Taken." An Introduction to American Poetry, edited by Lisa Swank, Viking Press, 2015, pp. 48-49.

Gallo, C. 2009. *The Presentation Secrets of Steve Jobs*. McGraw Hill.

Gallup and Lumina Foundation. 2024. *State of Higher Education 2024 Report*. Indianapolis: Lumina Foundation, May 2024. https://www.luminafoundation.org/wp-content/uploads/2024/05/State-of-Higher-Education-2024.pdf.

Ginsburg, Kenneth R. 2007. Committee on Communications, and Committee on Psychosocial Aspects of Child and Family Health. "The Importance of Play in Promoting Healthy Child Development and Maintaining Strong Parent-Child Bonds." *Pediatrics* 119, no. 1 (2007): 182-191.

Glasser, H., and M. Shay. 2025. "Market Analysis: A Problem Worth Solving." In *Clinical and Medical Innovation*, edited by Adam E.

M. Eltorai, Nancy Patterson, Sushrut S. Waikar, and Xixi Zhao, 31–43. *Innovation in Nephrology*. Academic Press, 2025. https://doi.org/10.1016/B978-0-323-95680-2.00023-5.

Gupta, V., I. C. MacMillan, and G. Surie. 2004. "Entrepreneurial Leadership: Developing and Measuring a Cross-Cultural Construct." *Journal of Business Venturing* 19, no. 2: 241–60. https://doi.org/10.1016/S0883-9026(03)00040-5.

Hannah, S. T., and B. J. Avolio. 2011. "Leader Character, Ethos, and Virtue: Individual and Collective Considerations." *Leadership Quarterly* 22, no. 5: 989–94.

Hannah, S. T., B. J. Avolio, and F. O. Walumbwa. 2011. "Relationships Between Authentic Leadership, Moral Courage, and Ethical and Pro-Social Behaviors." *Business Ethics Quarterly* 21, no. 4: 555–78. https://doi.org/10.5840/beq201121436.

Haynie, J. M., D. Shepherd, E. Mosakowski, and P. C. Earley. 2010. "A Situated Metacognitive Model of the Entrepreneurial Mindset." *Journal of Business Venturing* 25, no. 2: 217–29. https://doi.org/10.1016/j.jbusvent.2008.10.001.

Hinkin, T. R., and J. B. Tracey. 1999. "The Relevance of Charisma for Transformational Leadership in Stable Organizations." *Journal of Organizational Change Management* 12, no. 2: 105–19.

Hmieleski, K. M., and J. C. Carr. 2007. "The Relationship Between Entrepreneur Psychological Capital and Well-Being." *Frontiers of Entrepreneurship Research*.

Hmieleski, K. M., J. C. Carr, and R. A. Baron. 2015. "Integrating Discovery and Creation Perspectives of Entrepreneurial Action: The Relative Roles of Founding CEO Human Capital, Social Capital, and Psychological Capital in Contexts of Risk Versus Uncertainty." *Strategic Entrepreneurship Journal* 9, no. 4: 289–312. https://doi.org/10.1002/sej.1208.

Hoang, G., T. T. Luu, and M. T. Babalola. 2025. "Entrepreneurial Leadership: A Systematic Literature Review and Research Agenda." *Leadership & Organization Development Journal* 46, no. 2: 285–313. https://doi.org/10.1108/LODJ-05-2024-0350.

Hvide, H. K., and G. A. Panos. 2014. "Risk Tolerance and Entrepreneurship." *Journal of Financial Economics* 111, no. 1: 200–23. https://doi.org/10.1016/j.jfineco.2013.06.001.

International Monetary Fund. 2024. "World Economic Outlook Database." October. https://www.imf.org/en/Publications/WEO/weo-database/2024/October.

Isaacson, W. 2011. *Steve Jobs.* Simon & Schuster.

Jessup, L. M., and J. S. Valacich. 2019. "Growth, Adaptability, and Relationships Within the Changing Landscape of IS Education." *Journal of Information Systems Education* 30, no. 4: 217–21.

Kalshoven, K. H., D. N. Den Hartog, and A. H. B. De Hoogh. 2013. "Ethical Leadership and Follower Helping and Courtesy: Moral Awareness and Empathic Concern as Moderators." *Applied Psychology* 62, no. 2: 211–35. https://doi.org/10.1111/j.1464-0597.2011.00483.x.

Kelchen, R. 2023. *Examining the Effects of Tuition Controls on Student Enrollment.* June. https://robertkelchen.com/wp-content/uploads/2023/07/tuitioncontrol_enrollment_accepted.pdf.

Kezar, A., T. DePaola, and D. T. Scott. 2019. *The Gig Academy: Mapping Labor in the Neoliberal University.* Johns Hopkins University Press.

Kouzes, J. M., and B. Z. Posner. 2003. *Leadership Practices Inventory: LPI.* Pfeiffer.

Kouzes, T. K., and B. Z. Posner. 2019. "Influence of Managers' Mindset on Leadership Behavior." *Leadership & Organization Development Journal* 40, no. 8: 829–44.

Krueger, N. F. 2007. "What Lies Beneath? The Experiential Essence of Entrepreneurial Thinking." *Entrepreneurship Theory and Practice* 31, no. 1: 123–38. https://doi.org/10.1111/j.1540-6520.2007.00166.

Kuhn, T. S. 1997. *The Structure of Scientific Revolutions*. Vol. 962. University of Chicago Press.

Lawder, D. 2024. "US Small Business Surges, Sentiment Improves, Treasury Report Says." *Reuters*, September 4. https://www.reuters.com/markets/us/us-small-business-surges-sentiment-improves-treasury-report-says.2024-09-03/.

Lee, Jennifer. "Why Resilience Isn't Enough: The Case for Antifragile Leadership." *Fast Company*, April 18, 2025. https://www.fastcompany.com/91317307/why-resilience-isnt-enough-the-case-for-antifragile-leadership.

Leighton, Nick. 2021. "How to Cultivate an Ownership Mindset in Your Team." *Forbes*, November 22. https://www.forbes.com/councils/forbescoachescouncil/2021/11/22/how-to-cultivate-an-ownership-mindset-in-your-team/.

Lenarduzzi, V., and D. Taibi. 2016. "MVP Explained: A Systematic Mapping Study on the Definitions of Minimal Viable Product." In *2016 42th Euromicro Conference on Software Engineering and Advanced Applications (SEAA)*. IEEE.

Li, Y. N., K. S. Law, and M. Yan. 2019. "Other-Caring or Other-Critical? A Contagious Effect of Leaders' Emotional Triads on Subordinates' Performance." *Asia Pacific Journal of Management* 36: 995–1021. https://doi.org/10.1007/s10490-018-9617-5.

Liedtka, J. 2011. "Learning to Use Design Thinking Tools for Successful Innovation." *Strategy & Leadership* 39, no. 5: 13–9. https://doi.org/10.1108/10878571111161480.

Lin, W., H. Yin, and Z. Liu. 2022. "The Roles of Transformational Leadership and Growth Mindset in Teacher Professional Development: The Mediation of Teacher Self-Efficacy." *Sustainability* 14, no. 11: 6,489.

Majka, M. 2024. *Understanding Unique Value Proposition.* https://www.researchgate.net/profile/Marcin-Majka-2/publication/381917183_Understanding_Unique_Value_Proposition/links/668446702aa57f3b8268afa8/Understanding-Unique-Value-Proposition.pdf.

Marks, G. 2024. "Boomers are selling businesses to millennials in a generational handover." *The Guardian*, August 18. https://www.theguardian.com/business/article/2024/aug/18/small-business-boomer-millennial-wealth.

Marshall, P., and K. Barbour. 2015. "Making Intellectual Room for Persona Studies: A New Consciousness and a Shifted Perspective." *Persona Studies* 1, no. 1: 1–12.

Meinecke, A. L., and S. Kauffeld. 2018. "Engaging the Hearts and Minds of Followers: Leader Empathy and Language Style Matching During Appraisal Interviews." *Journal of Business Psychology* 34: 485–501. https://doi.org/10.1007/s10869-018-9554-9.

Meyer, Bertolt, Michael J. Burtscher, Klaus Jonas, et al. 2016. "What Good Leaders Actually Do: Micro-Level Leadership Behaviour, Leader Evaluations, and Team Decision Quality." *European Journal of Work and Organizational Psychology* 25, no. 6: 777–89. http://dx.doi.org/10.1080/1359432X.2016.1189903.

Miller, K. D. "Discernment in Management and Organizations." *Journal of Management, Spirituality & Religion* 17, no. 5 (2020): 373–402. https://doi.org/10.1080/14766086.2020.1812425.

Miller, M. 2009. "Transformational Leadership Behaviours and Empathy with Action." *Transformation* 26, no. 1: 45–59.

Muss, C., D. Tüxen, and B. Fürstenau. 2025. "Empathy in Leadership: A Systematic Literature Review on the Effects of Empathetic Leaders in Organizations." *Management Review Quarterly*. https://doi.org/10.1007/s11301-024-00472-7.

Neck, Heidi M., Christopher P. Neck, and Emma L. Murray. 2025. "Activating an Entrepreneurial Mindset." In *Entrepreneurship: The Practice and Mindset*, 3rd ed., 33–64. Thousand Oaks, CA: Sage.

Neessen, P. C. M., M. C. J. Caniëls, B. Vos, and J. P J. de Jong. 2019. "The Intrapreneurial Employee." *International Entrepreneurship and Management Journal* 15: 545–71. https://doi.org/10.1007/s11365-018-0552-1.

New York Post. 2024. "Gen Z More Likely than Their Parents, Grandparents to Be Entrepreneurs." August 19. https://nypost.com/2024/08/19/lifestyle/gen-z-more-likely-than-their-parents-grandparents-to-be-entrepreneurs/.

Priyaa, V. C. Praven, N. Kiruthika, A. Nivetha, P. P. Sajimon, Pankaj Singh Chandel, Ravi Kishor Agrawal, and P. Selvakumar. "Characteristics of Successful Entrepreneurs." In *Strategic Insights and Case Studies on Navigating an Entrepreneurial Landscape*, edited by Ponmalar N. Alagappar and Ramakrishna Yanamandra, 91–110. Hershey, PA: IGI Global Scientific Publishing, 2025. https://doi.org/10.4018/979-8-3693-9261-4.ch005.

Punjwani, M. 2024. "What Percentage of Startups Fail?" *Forbes*, October 23. https://www.forbes.com/advisor/business/software/startups-failure-rate/.

Putnam, L. L. 1979. "Preference for Procedural Order in Task-Oriented Small Groups." *Communications Monographs* 46, no. 3: 193–218.

Randall, K., M. Isaacson, and C. Ciro. (2017). "Validity and Reliability of the Myers-Briggs Personality Type Indicator: A Systematic Review and Meta-Analysis." *Journal of Best Practices in Health Professions Diversity* 10, no. 1: 1–27.

Renko, M., A. El Tarabishy, A. L. Carsrud, and M. Brännback. 2015. "Understanding and Measuring Entrepreneurial Leadership Style." *Journal of Small Business Management* 53, no. 1: 54–74. https://doi.org/10.1111/jsbm.12086.

Rigtering, J. P. C., and U. Weitzel. 2013. "Work Context and Employee Behaviour as Antecedents for Intrapreneurship." *International Entrepreneurship Management Journal* 9: 337–60.

Roberts, B. W., D. Wood, and J. L. Smith. 2005. "Evaluating Five Factor Theory and Social Investment Perspectives on Personality Trait Development." *Journal of Research in Personality* 39, no. 1: 166–84. https://doi.org/10.1016/j.jrp.2004.08.002.

Russ, S. W. 2016. "Pretend Play: Antecedent of Adult Creativity." *New Directions for Child and Adolescent Development* 2016, no. 151: 21–32.

Ryan, L. 2013. "Leading Change Through Creative Destruction: How Netflix's Self-Destruction Strategy Created Its Own Market." *International Journal of Business Innovation and Research* 7, no. 4: 429–445.

Singer, Dorothy G., Roberta Michnick Golinkoff, and Kathy Hirsh-Pasek. 2006. *Play = Learning: How Play Motivates and Enhances Children's Cognitive and Social-Emotional Growth*. Oxford University Press.

Sohmen, V. S. 2015. "Reflections on Creative Leadership." *International Journal of Global Business* 8, no. 1.

Tasneem, Afia. 2019. "What the Looming Demographic Storm Means for Your State." *EAB*, February 11. https://eab.com/resources/blog/enrollment-blog/what-the-looming-demographic-storm-means-for-your-state/.

Teare, G. 2024. "Global Funding Slowed in Q3, Even as AI Continued to Lead." *Crunchbase News*, October 3. https://news.crunchbase.com/venture/global-startup-funding-recap-q3-2024/.

Times Higher Education. 2023. "AI and Technology Disruption in Today's Higher Education Ecosystem." https://www.timeshighereducation.com/hub/consultancy/p/ai-and-technology-disruption-todays-higher-education-ecosystem.

Tversky, A., and D. Kahneman. 1974. "Judgment Under Uncertainty: Heuristics and Biases." *Science* 185, no. 4157: 1,124–31. https://doi.org/10.1126/science.185.4157.1124.

Uhl-Bien, M., and M. Arena. 2018. "Leadership for Organizational Adaptability: A Theoretical Synthesis and Integrative Framework." *Leadership Quarterly* 29, no. 1: 89–104.

United States Census Bureau. 2025. "Business Formation Statistics." February 12. https://www.census.gov/econ/bfs/.

US Small Business Administration Office of Advocacy. 2024. "New Advocacy Report Shows Small Business Total Reaches 34.8 Million, Accounting for 2.6 Million Net New Jobs in Latest Year of Data." November 19. https://advocacy.sba.gov/2024/11/19/new-advocacy-report-shows-small-business-total-reaches-34-8-million-accounting-for-2-6-million-net-new-jobs-in-latest-year-of-data/.

West, M. A., and A. W. Richter. 2024. "Climates and Cultures for Innovation and Creativity at Work." Edited by Zhou, Jing, and Christina E. Shalley. *Handbook of Organizational Creativity*. Psychology Press.

Williams, R. Jr., D. M. Raffo, and L. A. Clark. 2018. "Charisma as an Attribute of Transformational Leaders: What About Credibility?" *Journal of Management Development* 37, no. 6: 512–24.

World Intellectual Property Organization. 2024. "Global Innovation Index 2024: Switzerland, Sweden, US, Singapore, UK Top Ranking; China, Türkiye, India, Viet Nam, Philippines Among Fastest 10-Year Risers; Dark Clouds for Innovation Investments." September 26. https://www.wipo.int/pressroom/en/articles/2024/article_0013.html.

Young Entrepreneur Council. 2018. "The Importance of an Abundance Mindset for Business Leaders." *Inc.*, January 2. https://www.inc.com/young-entrepreneur-council/the-importance-of-an-abundance-mindset-for-business-leaders.html.